AF218000

Dear My Teacher

*Letters of joy, pain, and triumph
from today's teenage Hmong students*

EDITED & COMPILED BY

PANG YANG
MIKE H. VANG

HMONG EDUCATIONAL RESOURCES

PUBLISHER

Published by Hmong Educational Resources (HER) Publisher, LLC, 2019.

Hmong Educational Resources is an independent publisher of books by or about Hmong. HER is a one of a kind publishing company that provides services for Hmong students, writers, educators, researchers, and graphic artists.
HER publishes books in a wide range of categories and formats, fiction and non-fiction, and for audiences of all ages and educational backgrounds.
For more information about HER Publisher, please contact Dr. Brian V. Xiong by phone at (612) 978-8359 or email at hmongeducationalresources@gmail.com.

Dear My Teacher edited and compiled by Pang Yang and Mike H. Vang.
Additional editing by Brian Xiong.
Designed by Fue Yang.

Hmong Educational Resources Publisher, Saint Paul, MN, 2019
ISBN: 978-1-64410-004-2

This book is dedicated to my students.

When I look into each of your eyes, it reflects who I was when I was young. I see amazing, resilient, and talented individuals with hearts of gold waiting to be pumped-up! Discover your identity to find your passion, so you can courageously walk into the world confidently.

I'm so proud of you!

~Ms. Yang~

Preface

THIS BOOK IS A COLLABORATION BETWEEN THE HMONG for Native Speakers classes at Park Center Senior High and Osseo Senior High, located in the Osseo Area School District. The students' letters in this book were written to us, their teachers, with the hope that by sharing their feelings on paper, we may benefit from seeing the world through their eyes. These letters are anonymous to ensure they are written authentically and straight from the heart. Some proper nouns were changed to protect the identity of the students.

Osseo Area Schools is in the Northwest suburbs of the Twin Cities serving all or parts of Brooklyn Center, Brooklyn Park, Corcoran, Dayton, Maple Grove, Osseo, Plymouth, and Rogers. It's the fifth largest school district with the second largest Hmong population, second to Saint Paul Public Schools. With over 20,000 students and 80 dialects spoken by students, the diverse background of students enriches experiences in the classroom. We currently offer Spanish and Hmong for Native Speakers classes to our students at both Osseo Senior High and Park Center Senior High. Please visit www.district279.org to find out more about our schools and district.

Osseo Senior High is located at the junction of three major cities coming together, in the northwest corner of the Twin Cities Metro area: Maple Grove, Brooklyn Park and Osseo. Like its physical location, Osseo Senior High (OSH) is home to the Osseo Orioles, a junction point where students, staff and families from diverse backgrounds and walks of life, come together and commit to working collectively toward a common mission that "inspires and prepares all students with the confidence, courage, and competence to achieve their dreams, contribute to community; and engage in a lifetime of learning," (Osseo Area Schools-District 279).

Furthermore, OSH embodies the vibrant features of its mascot's namesake, the Oriole. From the leadership of Principal, Michael Lehan, to the exuberant demeanor of the newest staff members, OHS has a deep commitment towards the celebration of its colorful learning community and puts great emphasis on cultural competency in its delivery of academic modalities. Indicative to such commitment is OSH's successful launch of the Native Hmong class. In its first year, Native Hmong touts an at-capacity enrollment number of 35 students, despite being offered as an elective course in the Word Language Department.

As of today, the OSH Hmong for Native Speakers class mirrors the success of its big sister, the Hmong for Native Speakers classes at Park Center Senior High (PCSH) in Brooklyn Park, and it's showing early signs of high demands for future expansion in the number of course sections offered to students, for the subsequent years to come.

Park Center Senior High is a first ring suburban high school located northwest of Minneapolis led by Principal Heather Miller-Cink. We're a diverse group of students and staff, including Hmong, Liberian, Hispanic, Vietnamese, and many more. One goal of our comprehensive high school is to provide a culturally responsive and differentiated curriculum of strong rigor in a caring environment with the expectation that all students will succeed. Park Center Senior High has over 400 Hmong students in attendance, over 20% of the student population.

This is our second year offering the Hmong for Native Speakers courses at Park Center. There are now six full classes offered for students. Next year, students will be able to take Hmong for Native Speakers at level I, II, or III. We have worked hard to create this rigorous course and are very proud of the culturally relevant experiences that it offers.

This special book is made possible by the Education Minnesota Foundation Classroom Grant: The Untold Story. The format of this book is organized into three sections: Self-Discovery, Health, and Family. Although many letters do overlap in themes, we selected one section to put each letter in. We hope you enjoy the letters straight from the minds, hearts, and souls of Hmong high school students. We would like to thank our Instructional Coach, Angie Vivatson, and retired teaching colleague, Katherine Hutchinson, for your countless hours editing this book to make it publishable. Last but not least, Mr. Sing Ly, for your continued support to heal the hearts of students who believe in you.

PANG YANG

MIKE VANG

ANGIE VIVATSON

Table of Contents

Table of Contents

V

Table of Contents

Introduction

By Pang Yang

THE BIRTH OF THIS BOOK WAS A RESULT OF THE EXPERIENCES I had as an introverted Hmong student growing up in an American K-12 education system in Minnesota. I was on a search all my life to find my voice in order to share my life experiences with the people around me. Our Hmong-American students are a reflection of who I was, and to have their stories be told is to open the world of the unknown. This book demonstrates how to open a can of worms, face the fears, and be able to move on with grace and insight.

It took almost half of my life to find who I am, for the experiences I had to endure shaped who I am today as a teacher, a mother, a wife, a daughter, and a Hmong daughter-in-law. I no longer have to be 50% American and 50% Hmong because I have finally learned to balance my life living as a Hmong-American and keep my own identity alive.

During my high school years, my worst fear was to have my teachers judging me because 99% of my teachers didn't look like me. What would they think of me if I told them about parts of my life that I was ashamed of? How would they react? Would they be able to understand what I was going through because they are not from my ethnic background? Would they tell my story to other students? Could I trust them? I had a million questions and no answers.

As an adult in my early thirties, I reflected upon my experiences in school, especially the silence in my undergraduate program where I was left out of group discussions and at times felt invisible because I was an introvert and didn't speak up. My college classmates, 98% of whom were White, would sometimes look back and forth at each other and have discussions and not even one would look at me or ask me, "What do you think?" This not only happened once, but countless times. It hurts to reflect on the past and it hurts to not be seen. That is when I realized the power of speaking from within: to ask for understanding, to ask for help, or to ask for anything. The worst thing someone could say is "NO." I finally found my voice after all these years. I often interject in conversations and ask questions for clarification or curiosity. I don't want to be that invisible student all over again and miss the opportunity for my voice to be heard.

I have learned to speak my truth, so that I don't keep my experiences inside of me buried in my baggage. My baggage has been so full of racial encounters, microaggressions in the workplace, and so much more that have been buried for so long, but I didn't have a single safe place to unpack it until Courageous Conversation trainings by Glen Singleton became a part of my district's professional development. By participating in the sessions and practicing these skills, I learned to speak my truth. I learned to talk about one of the hardest things in life that we barely talk about: RACE. As a Hmong daughter, my family never had conversations about race. We just didn't talk about it; many Hmong families still don't talk about it today. To accept non-closure in the hardest conversations and to feel discomfort was hard, but it was part of the journey to finally heal from the inside and to find liberation.

What you should know is that our Hmong-American students, including those who were born in Thailand or Laos and immigrated to the United States (generation 1.5), as well as students who were born in the U.S. to immigrant and/or refugee parents (generation 2.0) and students whose grandparents came to the U.S. in the 1970s and 80s (generation 3.0), the generation 1.5 students are quite different than students from generation 3.0 in Hmong language proficiency. These differences in generations make our class unique and provides opportunities for everyone to learn from one another.

Students wouldn't be comfortable sharing personal information (what is under the iceberg), but Mike and I spent many days at the beginning of the school year gaining students' trust through community building activities, being vulnerable about our own life experiences, leading lessons around race, and being real. We have to be open-minded and listen to what our Hmong-American students have to say because sometimes they just want to be heard. You should also note that some letters are written in Hmong because students have the ability to express their feelings in their native tongue.

I discovered the letter idea in a blog two summers ago. I wrote my own authentic letter to my English high school teacher pretending I was in high school all over again. As I read this letter aloud in my classes, students could hear the changes in my voice. It took power to share this letter. Even though I experienced these events 20 plus years ago, it still feels like yesterday. Here is my example letter:

JUNE 1, 1994

Dear Teacher,

This has been a bittersweet journey for 12 years in the Saint Paul Public School system. I'm so grateful to share this with you, someone who would listen and wanted to see me for who I really am. This has allowed me to share the private world that I was living in.

I have been that quiet Hmong student in your class with perfect attendance, who was always respectful and did her homework for the last 12 years from first grade until now. I was that introverted kid who never questioned you, but instead, I was burning inside because I was desperate to learn, so that I could have a chance at the American dream. There is so much you don't know about me that I wish you knew. Since you asked, I hope you will not judge me for what I'm about to share. Not a single teacher has wanted to know more about the girl who was the imperfect A student until now. Three things I wished you knew about me were:

First and foremost, my father just divorced my mother on paper last year so that he could marry another young wife from Laos, two years younger than me. I believe he was one of the very first to commit this action in our community. I was sickened and so devastated; only my friends could heal my soul. I cried endlessly with my mom each night knowing that we may never be together again as one family. Each night I wept in bed knowing that my life was over, and my family was going to be torn apart because of my father's action. What was wrong with him? I had no answers, and I wished he wasn't my father. I asked myself why my father would do what he did, for I felt he no longer loved my siblings or me because he didn't love our mother.

Secondly, I wish you knew that over and over, I had people who didn't believe in me when I told them I had big dreams. My counselor told me to go to a community college when I told her I was applying to a private university. She said I wasn't ready for the private school challenges, and that I was better off at a community college. I was upset that she didn't support me, but didn't have words to express my frustration to my parents or anyone else. I watched some of teachers favor the 'A' students (teacher's pets), while I struggled with adult responsibilities: working two part-time jobs, being a mother figure to my four younger siblings after school because my mom worked second-shift with two jobs at $4 an hour, cleaning and cooking nightly at home, and helping my father run his own Chinese restaurant by working another 18 hours on weekends. Despite all this, I still earned a place on the "B" honor roll. I probably juggled more tasks than an average teen. While my White peers were playing sports, going to school dances, and watching football games, I was becoming an adult and gaining life-long skills.

Lastly, I wish I had teachers who looked like me, those who knew what it felt like to be hungry when there wasn't enough food to eat at the end of the month, and how it felt to live in two cultures while trying to meet the high expectations at home and at the same time discovering what it means to be American. I wish I had teachers who knew how hard it was to be a student of color in the educational system, so that they could have showed me the easier road ahead. I hungered for life skills from my teachers, but no one bothered to share any life experiences to make the road ahead of me easier.

By reading this letter, you give me hope. I have hope that you will be the change in my future. I hope that you will listen with an open heart and mind and give me a hug at times when I want to cry in class. Maybe you could just read my daily journal? Every single word of heartache is there, but all that you do is put a check mark and turn the pages.

Sincerely,
The Introvert

5

Many Hmong-Americans are lost in the educational institution because they are assumed to be the "model minority." They are introverts, often keeping their own thoughts to themselves. They don't act out in class; instead, they simply comply with teacher instructions and requests. At home, these students are fighting an internal battle between how to uphold Hmong values and at the same time be that top-notch Asian model minority students that their parents expect them to be. Hmong students have an opportunity that their parents didn't have; therefore, their success represents both their own and that of their parents. That is a lot of pressure for a young Hmong adult. On the inside, students are slowly melting away and dying to figure out life and find their own path. They are hoping someone will lend an ear to listen to them. They are just waiting for that push from someone to help them come out of their shell, to overcome an obstacle. They simply can't just get over it, as it takes time to internalize and heal.

According to the Pew Research, the U.S. Hmong population has a 53% high school diploma or less educational attainment. Only 14% of Hmong-Americans have bachelor's degree compared to 30% of all Asian American bachelor's degree attainment. These statistics are important to understand when seeing the larger picture of the impact of educational attainment in the Hmong community in terms of poverty (Figure 1).

FOR EDUCATIONAL INSTITUTIONS

Unlike Wisconsin and California where the Hmong are dispersed across the state, the majority of Hmong in Minnesota reside in the Twin Cities, which makes it unique and provides the potential for power in numbers. Educational institutions must provide and fully fund culturally-relevant education for students. Curriculum courses could include Heritage/History, Ethnic Studies, Language Arts and Literature from the Hmong language and cultural perspective. In addition, departments should collabo-

% OF U.S. HMONG POPULATION LIVING IN POVERTY, 2015

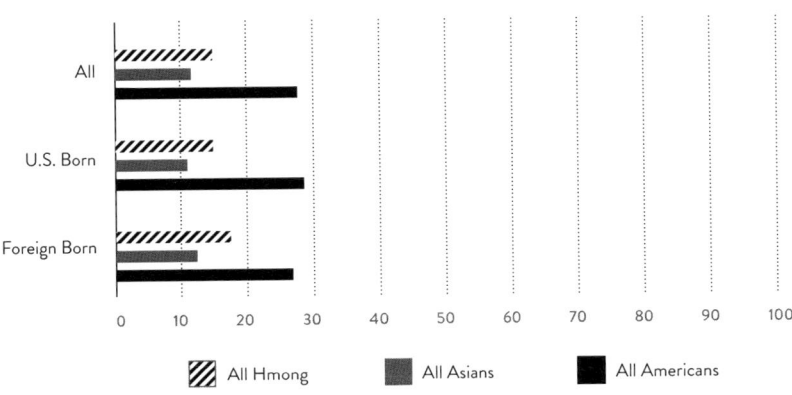

FIGURE 1: Pew Research Statistics (2015)

TOP 10 U.S. METROPOLITAN AREAS BY HMONG POPULATION, 2015

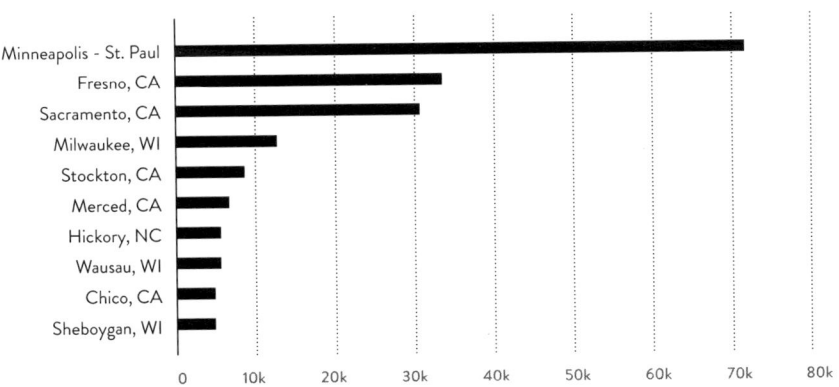

FIGURE 2: Pew Research Statistics (2015)

rate to bring courses alive through culturally relevant hands-on learning.

School communities need to look more like the students they serve. School districts need to actively recruit and retain teachers, administrators, and support staff of a broad range of minority groups. School need to be sensitive to the cultural needs of the student population, especially in the food choices served at breakfast and lunch. This is both respectful and interesting to the student body at large.

Simply having Hmong-American students graduate from high school is no longer acceptable. The bigger picture shows greater disparity in the Hmong community in terms of economic wealth, poverty, health disparities, home ownership, and educational attainment, according to multiple organizations leading the work to have healthier communities such as the Coalition for Asian American Leaders. If Hmong-American adult students are graduating from high school, but they are facing more obstacles than their Asian counterparts and don't have the skills, tools, and resources to overcome the obstacles, we, as K-12 educational systems haven't set them up for success, but failure. Because of this we no longer can clump all ethnic minorities into one large racial category, but must disaggregate data in education, health, housing, and economics to help us see the holistic picture of each ethnic community. This will allow us to focus on the special needs of the community.

In many conversations, my Asian colleagues and I have noticed that the focus is on Black and Brown students, often omitting others. I remind you to not forget about "other" students who are struggling to find themselves because one size doesn't necessarily work for all. We must bring parents, students, and community organizations to the table to shed light and bring more innovative ideas to reach all students.

FOR EDUCATORS

Read the letters in this book with your heart, not with judgement for the Hmong students who sits in front of you. Hopefully the stories here inspire you to see those who are most quiet in your classroom, and remember they too have a story to tell and needs that must be met. As teachers, we must not only teach the content, but to give ourselves permission at times to go off the written curriculum map, and develop deeper authentic relationships with our students, even if it means being vulnerable, such as sharing our own failures in life. No one is perfect. The openness of your journey in life will allow your students to appreciate you more and build connections at a deeper level. Students may not tell you that now, but when they reach adulthood and reflect, you will be the one they will remember most. For the students who spoke on mental health topics in their letters, we were able to connect them to experts in the school building that can help students address their mental health needs.

Secondly, I want you to remember Chimamanda Ngozi Adichie's presentation, *The Danger of a Single Story*, from TEDGlobal 2009 presentation:

All of these stories make me who I am. But to insist on only these negative stories is to flatten my experience and to overlook the many other stories that formed me. The single story creates stereotypes, and the problem with stereotypes is not that they are untrue, but that they are incomplete. They make one story become the only story.... I've always felt that it's impossible to engage properly with a place or a person without engaging with all of the stories of that place and that person. The consequence of the single story is this: It robs people of dignity. It makes our recognition of our equal humanity difficult. It emphasizes how we're different rather than how we're similar... Stories matter. Many stories matter. Stories have been used to dispossess and to malign, but stories can also be used to empower and to humanize. Stories can break the dignity of a people, but stories can also repair that broken dignity....I would like to end with this thought: That when we reject the single story, when we realize that there is never a single story about any place, we regain a kind of paradise (TED Ideas Worth Spreading, 2009).

This is a careful reminder of the uniqueness of each of our students. Each is multifaceted with a shared, but varied history. Each student comes with their own strengths (and weaknesses), skills, vision and personality. We all know this as teachers: this makes the spicy life of a classroom. In the drive to empathize and understand we generalize. I ask you to resist this. View our students in the abundance they bring to us.

HMONG PARENTS

This book is meant to mend relationships that have been broken and strengthen those relationships that exist. Read to open your mind and understand the complexity of our Hmong students in the 21st century. I often hear Hmong parents say, "How come Hmong kids these days are not like us in the past?" Hmong teens today are not supposed to be like you. Our Hmong students today live in a complex world with social media influences and must navigate different paths compared to past generations. They are the new "us." When I asked my high school Hmong students what can parents do to build better and stronger relationships with their young adult, here in this book, in their own world, is what students want to say.

Many Hmong students tell me, the toughest thing for them is to live with their parents' high expectations without their parents' support and understanding. The anxiety that flows into their minds with their parents' expectations of them becoming doctors and lawyers, has caused them to give up. It's great to have high expectations for our teens, but continue to listen to your teens' desires to achieve their dreams and their career choices. Give them the continued support (not just verbally, but physically, mentally, and emotionally) to help guide them to select the best pathway for a successful future.

Many times, our Hmong-American teens are expected to act like grown-ups helping to take care of younger siblings. At the same time, we must remember that they are still young and want to experience being a teenager. Some students have expressed their fear in becoming adults when they feel unprepared and have anxiety about their unknown future. As parents, you can help them by becoming that bridge to adulthood. They need your guidance and look up to you. A simple talk with them can help ease anxiety. A simple, "I'm sorry" can go along way towards mending broken relationships. This may be hard to do because some more traditional Hmong parents don't apologize to their children because of cultural norms.

Another suggestion that is key to bonding closer relationship is having a growth mindset. As parents, we have used motivational techniques, but often it sends the wrong message. We sometimes tell stories of our younger years, give lectures, and at time compare our young adults to others in hopes to motivate, but reserve psychology no longer works. Young adults may become discouraged and give up. A psychologist, Dr. Carol Dweck, says, "In a growth mindset, people believe that their most basic abilities can be developed through dedication and hard work. This view creates a love of learning and a resilience that is essential for great accomplishment. Virtually all people who achieved top performance had these qualities" (Mindset Works, Inc., 2017). Praising young adults for their efforts will help them foster a growth mindset.

Because some of us were raised in a culture without hugs or the words, "I love you," our children are hungry for love - verbally, emotionally, and physically. Reverse psychology in which we scold our teens like our parents scolded us, so they would work harder and do better, no longer works with the current Hmong-American youth. The more we use negative words, the farther they drift away from us.

As an educator, I truly believe in the power of a strong relationship with each child up through adulthood. The teenage years are so crucial to the mental health and success of your child. Even with seven children of my own, each child is so unique in their own ways, and I need to nurture all of them differently. My students over and over say that the second thing that pulls them down is when parents compare them to another person, whether it's another sibling or cousin. Comparison not only makes children disapprove of themselves, but they lose hope and give up because of the feeling of not being as good as their older sibling or an aunt makes them shut down completely.

I believe our generation has dropped the ball on becoming better parents. Some followed our parents' footsteps in leaving their child's complete future to educators because they are considered the "experts." In the 21st century, we can no longer leave it up to the schools. We must work together with our children's educators to bring out their brilliance, so they can succeed everywhere. The young, Hmong adults I work with want and need their parents' and guardians' support to succeed. They want closer relationships with their parents and guardians and they want to be loved. I hope after reading this book, you are ready to begin or continue your journey to develop an even stronger relationship with your child(ren) and make the time to collaborate with schools because you can't do this work alone. Together we can go farther.

In the last ten years, it's more prevalent that there is a widening educational gap between the males and females in the Hmong community. Now more than ever, Hmong women are achieving higher education degrees, and some have chosen to marry outside of the Hmong community because of various reasons. Young Hmong men have been brought up by values held by our parents' generation on gender roles, giving them more time to relax, and less parental control. As a result, these Hmong boys have fewer responsibilities and obtain fewer skills compared to our young Hmong women. Because of how some young Hmong men have been raised, they tend to struggle more with multi-tasking, time management, and struggle to live up to the Hmong society expectations during adulthood. The stresses of not being able to carry the torch, whether that is cultural traditions, language, or clan name, gives young Hmong men a sense of failure. In the end, I have seen more and more young Hmong men take on gaming as a form of stress relief from society's pressures.

Last but not least, the mental health needs of our Hmong students have been a taboo subject in our community. Mental health has been negatively viewed and at times not spoken of or even acknowledged because of the stigma in our community. The social-emotional needs of Hmong youth are so important to their success in school and in life; therefore, can't be ignored. Relationship is key and getting professional help is necessary to move students forward with mental health needs.

MY STUDENTS

As I read your stories, your words hit my emotions with tears drip-dropping one by one. You are so articulate, expressing your inner thoughts straight from your heart, pouring out what has been on your minds for years and being able to bring the deepest wounds on paper. Each time I read them, my eyes were filled with tears, wishing I could hold each of you in my arms and tell you everything would be just fine. For some of you, I know this was a very emotional assignment, but I also hope it brings closure to the old you and a new you will become of it.

For some, you no longer have to live in complete darkness, sadness, and pain. I hope parents, relatives, friends and educators who read your stories and see a deeper side of you for who you are. I know this is only a small glimpse into your life. There are many more life stories for you to share with me, your friends, your families, and people you meet along the way. My hope for you is no more loneliness, for tomorrow will bring you new friendships and closer relationships. Every adult in this school and in your life is committed to helping you achieve your highest potential. All you have to do is ask, just like you have asked Mr. Vang and me.

As you become more empowered and confident, the introvert in you will transform you into a new person. It just takes time to come out of your shell before your best is put forward. We look forward to seeing you fly into the unknown. You are the world to me. I'm reminded everyday why I still teach. Everyday I come to work to inspire you or be inspired by you. You remind me of my younger self and the youthfulness I still have inside. You give me hope because I know that inside each one of you there is a stronger person. As Hmong-American youth, you are resilient in obstacles that come before you. Our rich history from China to Laos to America is a testimony to our resiliency as a people. Because of this you have the opportunity to do anything you can dream and follow your passion. Never give up. Dream BIG. Go and show the world what you are all about. We will celebrate your successes along the way.

Thank you for sharing your authentic self in hopes of bringing understanding, new insights and change. I know your experiences will bring change to our families, our schools and the larger community. Your story is a voice for a better tomorrow.

Enjoy reading.

Self-Discovery

A LITTLE TOO LATE

Dear Teacher,

I live in Brooklyn Park with my parents and siblings, sometimes with my grandma and grandpa. The reason I say this is because my grandparents are always traveling, and they would come home for a week and then leave. Most of the time they are in Wisconsin where my grandpa's family is currently living. Before I came to this school, I attended a middle school for one year, and then transferred to a Hmong charter school and back to the same middle school again. I'm a ninth grader, and I'm here to tell you about things I want you to know.

I attended a Hmong charter school in seventh grade. I was a typical quiet Hmong student and not that smart. I failed most of the exams and didn't pay much attention to my homework. I guess my teachers thought badly of me. Few of my classmates tried to help me at school, but later they decided not to hangout with me that much anymore because it appeared that I was a troublemaker in front of everyone. I decided to change, and I guess that change only made things worse. I began to hate everyone because I was labeled as a troublemaker, a failure, and a delinquent. I started to hang out with the wrong group and did all the wrong stuff. My mother would try to help and guide me to the right path, but I guess I didn't take her words seriously. I was careless; I had no sympathy and no empathy for others.

That is what it was like on the outside, but on the inside I was dying because I cared so much. I wanted to do good so others can see a better me besides a tough delinquent student. Teachers would look down at me as I walked in the hallway or as I entered their classes. As times passed by, the good person I was inside started to fade away.

Then eighth grade came. At that time, I was emotionless because my cousins and brothers tried to help, but I would just tell them that

I was alright, too afraid of telling them the truth. Near the end of the school year, the teachers told us that all of the students would be given a task to write a graduation speech. I wasn't stunned at all about this graduation speech. I was a failure, so when I was given the paper to write down what I had to say, I thought, "What the heck! It's the end of the school year, so I might as well give it a try." I did my best and after a few weeks a teacher pulled me from my class. I thought I was in trouble and all of my friends thought I was in trouble, but when I got to the hall, the teacher told me that I was one of the three students chosen to give a graduation speech; I was confused, unsure, and scared. She gave me a choice to either take the opportunity or to decline it. I told her I needed time to think about it because in my head I was thinking, "How could I be one of the three students out of 120 students to be chosen?" I thought they had the wrong guy.

That same day I decided that I was going to take it. The teacher was glad I took it, but I was scared. No, I was petrified because I had never done anything like this before. So, when I got home I was scared to tell my parents, but when I did share the good news, they were happy. My father laughed with joy, but since I was so full of negativity, I took it the wrong way and I started to get mad. I was mad how they wanted me to wear a suit and everything, and mad that all they did was laugh. I turned the tables and made everything worse; I emailed the teacher that I wasn't going to do it anymore My father and my mother were both mad; my brothers and sisters told me that I would regret not taking the opportunity. I was disappointed in myself.

Graduation day arrived. We were all walking down and doing our thing. When they announced the graduation speakers, they announced two students who were going to give a graduation speech, and then they announced the third person, who was supposed to be me, but they called a different student's name. I was sad at that point, but I told myself that it's done, and it's over. To this day, I still regret not taking the opportunity to shine.

Sincerely,
A Little Too Late

A PART OF ME DOESN'T WANT TO GROW UP

Dear Teacher,

Hi, I'm 15 years old, and I will be turning 16 soon. I really don't like talking about my future, or what I want to do in the future because it's such a sensitive topic to talk about with me. The thought of growing up has now finally hit me. When I was young, I wanted to grow up fast to become an adult, and now it has finally come true. It's really scary. I don't want to go college because I don't know what I want to major in. I feel like I do need to go, so I can succeed early and start making money for my future plans; however, a part of me doesn't want to go to college. The thought of going to school again, and how broken our society is scares me. For example, the information we learn in school, I feel is unnecessary for me.

I have dreams, but they are not enough to satisfy my parents, especially my dad. I don't want to be a doctor or major in Information Technology or anything that involves the medical field, or just something basic that everyone wants to do. My aunt is going to be a Pharmacist and is still aiming for it; yes, I'm really proud of her, but all my dad talks about is how he wants me to be like her and I don't want to because it's just not my thing. I like to be different and that 'different' is that I really like art or just something that involves music that allows me to be myself and have a way to express who I really am. I want to just go into the music industry, but really I don't think that is going to happen. That is why I need to find what my plan B is before it's too late.

Teacher, I think I'm just a lost person in general. I'm just all over the place with focusing on what I like to do right now, and it has nothing to do with what is really important and going to help me in life. I always get in my own way of things, and I give up because I don't know what to do. I would work on it for a few days, feeling proud of how far I have gotten. Then the next day I just feel down, and I forget what I was working on and end my motivation. I really need to train myself to get used to it because if I never do it and don't have that mindset, I don't think it will ever happen. Someday, I will not have my parents holding my hands anymore, guiding me through tough obstacles. All of the times when I want to run away from home or I just get so excited to leave, I don't think I can because of how scared I am. I finally understand and think that my parents were sometimes right, and of course wrong too because I do have my own opinions. I need to start planning. I really don't want to regret anything, so as of right now I will plan and live happily. I don't think I will ever satisfy my parents, but as long I'm happy and feel like I have made it, I will not stop.

Sincerely,
A Part of Me Doesn't Want to Grow Up

FUTURE *QEEJ* MASTER

Dear Teacher,

The first thing I wish that you knew about me is that my family and I had moved quite a lot back then. I decided to stay as an ambivert because I have a decent number of friends here. I decided not to have a lot of friends because I would probably have to leave them just like when I moved from California to Minnesota. For the meanwhile I'm trying to make some friends, but at the same time I'm not really trying. I'm actually pretty talkative if you know me well.

The second thing I want you to know is that I take a lot of interest in Hmong culture and our history. I like knowing about our culture the most, so that when I'm older I already know what to do at specific events. I want our culture to continue and not die off, so I like learning about Hmong people and the culture. I know a lot about our Hmong history from my parents and other people such as a *qeej* master named Mr. Her. From the first day of learning how to master the musical arts of the *qeej*, the Hmong culture didn't really suit my interests. One day, my dad took me with my brother to learn and before I knew it, I was almost done with learning about the *qeej*. Later on, I just started to like playing the *qeej* and attending a lot of funerals. In those three years of learning, I have made tons of friends who were like brothers to me and traveled a lot with them.

Lastly, I want you to know that I go to funerals quite often, so I understand the basics and more. Back in California I would literally go to funerals almost every weekend with my brother and friends. Sometimes my friends and I would travel 2-3 hours to go to funerals. Also, I have been to a relative's funeral in Wisconsin and in Minnesota with my brother to help play the *qeej*. Throughout my life as a *tub qeej*, I believe that helping the Hmong community and continuing our tradition is my main priority.

Growing up in a strict family, I have faced many ups and downs to keep my tradition and culture alive. Basically, I live in two separate worlds. Living as a Hmong boy learning all about who I really am, and also living as an American student who wants to chase the American dream. Living as a Hmong American and trying to become a *qeej* master to keep my culture alive while aiming to be an engineer trying to help our American society grow, is my dream. I want to be a Hmong American boy that can connect Hmong children and Hmong elders together. I want to be that bridge that holds the foundation of the American dreams and Hmong dreams.

Sincerely,
Future Qeej Master

QUIET HMONG PRIDE

Dear Teacher,
You probably know me as that shy and quiet girl in class who has nothing to say, but I have to tell you that is not the case. As you know, the quiet ones are always the ones that have a lot to say. I just wanted to let you know that you should not only pay attention to the students who speak a lot, but also the students who have little to say. I feel that you know less about the quiet students more than the students who speak a lot. Since, I'm one of those quiet students, these are three things I wished you knew about me.

The first thing I wished you knew about me is that I don't understand my native Hmong language. When I say I don't understand Hmong, I literally don't. This means I need subtitles whenever a Hmong person speaks to me. Growing up, my mom never really spoke Hmong to my siblings and me. She always spoke English to us. There are times where she did try to teach us Hmong, but we just wouldn't understand at all. Besides, my step-dad is not Hmong, and the only way for all of us to communicate with each other was by speaking English. Also, I didn't grow up around the Hmong community. At a young age, my family and I moved to North Carolina, and I basically spent my whole childhood life there. North Carolina doesn't have a lot of Hmong people living there. In that case, the area I lived in didn't have Hmong people at all. I went to a school that, of course, had only English speakers. The sad part about not knowing Hmong was when my friends would ask me to say something in my native language, but I wouldn't know how to answer because I didn't even know how to speak Hmong. Also, another sad part was that I didn't even know about my own culture. Nothing at all. When my family and I moved back to Minnesota in 2013, I found it hard to fit in with the Hmong community because I didn't understand what they would say, or the things they do in the culture. I felt like I didn't even belong in my own community. To this day I still find it a little bit hard to fit in with the Hmong community.

The second thing I wished you knew about me is that I'm a huge fan of the Korean boys band called BTS. You probably think I'm the typical fangirl, but I can't tell you how much BTS has impacted my life. BTS are artists that have changed the lives of so many around the world. They are the most inspirational, motivational, loving, considerate, and hardworking people I have ever seen in my life. They talk about serious topics, such as suicide, depression, anxiety, low self-esteem, and basically things that caused the youth to be insecure of their true selves. BTS always tells their fans and haters to love themselves and to speak for themselves.

Whenever I'm sad or mad, I listen to their music, and it cheers me up and calms me down. They helped me learn to love myself and helped me find my own voice. BTS makes me happy, and they are one out of the two most motivational people in my life that helps me strive to move forward after God. No matter what, they will always be my favorite boys band.

The last thing I wish you knew about me is I'm very artistic. I love to draw human portraits and anime. Also, I like to crochet, knit, play piano and ukulele, sing, and dance. I do all these things whenever I have free time, as a hobby or just for fun. I'm not the best at any of these things, but I just enjoy doing them!

In conclusion, I'm that shy and quiet girl in class who has little to say. I hope you learned a few things about me, and I hope you know that the three things I wished you knew about me are the three things that made me into the person I am today. Please remember to also pay attention to the quiet students because they have a lot to say too! Thank you for reading this!

Sincerely,
Quiet Hmong Pride

THANKFUL K-POP FAN

Dear Teacher,

You probably know me as the quiet Asian girl who sits in the front row of class. The Asian girl who keeps to herself, the Asian girl with poofy hair, and the Asian girl who gets good grades. Yes, all of that is true. I admit that. But that doesn't mean that is everything about me, and you probably already know that. So, I'm here to tell you three things I wished you knew about me!

The first thing I wished you knew about me is that I'm a K-Pop fanatic! I'm not over exaggerating. I really enjoy listening to Korean music. I love how the beat, the singing, and the dancing all flow well together. To keep it short, K-Pop is Korean pop music. K-Pop consists of tons of boy groups and girl groups; these groups are like your NSync and Backstreet Boys groups. The only difference is that they are Asian. The reason why I really enjoy K-Pop is because it makes me happy. It makes me want to dance, laugh, and cry. K-Pop has been with me since I was little, and I have been with it ever since. I don't think it's leaving my side anytime soon. I remember my first K-Pop crush. His name was G-Dragon aka Kim Jiyong. He is another story that I will tell you next time. Anyways, K-Pop has always just been next to me. Without K-Pop, I don't ever think I would know the people I know today, and I would have never been able to be a fangirl over those talented human beings.

Other than wanting you to know that I'm a K-Pop fanatic, I wish you knew that I value my family very much. It sounds cliché, but without my family, I have no idea what life would be like. Who would nag me about cleaning and cooking? What siblings would I be able to annoy 24-7? Nobody. Without my parents, siblings, uncles, aunts, etc., the list could go on and on, but without them, I wouldn't have the memories I have today. I always love attending family gatherings because I get to see everyone. I get to see all the babies crying, running around the house, and being crazy. I get to see the boys play their video games. I get to see the girls play "chef" or "house" outside. I get to see everyone and everything. Although they are crazy and make me mad, they will always hold a special place in my heart.

Finally, the last thing I wished you knew about me is that I appreciate you. It may not seem like it because I'm quiet and don't talk to you as often, but I do appreciate you. You work the hardest you can, and I see that. I see your effort when you try to make things fun and make the lessons understandable. I see your passion about what you teach; there is like a sparkle in your eye. You try your best to keep students calm, and you try your best to understand them. I can tell that all you want for your students is to live for who they are. You want to make students' lives as best as you can, to the best of your abilities. When students need help, you want to push them and keep pushing them. I can go on and on about how much I appreciate you, but that would take centuries. Just remember that I truly appreciate the things you do for me, my classmates, and other students.

You probably already knew me as the quiet Asian girl, but now you know three more things about your quiet Asian student. Now, you know that I'm a K-Pop fanatic, that I value my family, and that I appreciate you. There are a ton of other things that I wished you knew, but because I can only choose three, you only get those three. Always feel free to ask me if you want to know more. I know I only wrote a little, but I hoped you enjoyed.

Sincerely,
Thankful K-Pop Fan

FREQUENTLY ABSENT

Dear Teacher,

At times I can be a loud and outgoing person. I used to be like that all the time, but now I have forced myself into being an introvert. I battle all the time with self-doubt, sometimes depression, mostly anxiety, etc., but nothing too out of the ordinary. I don't have many problems, and I don't like to complain too much, so I keep to myself. I always thought being like that would make me safe, but it seems like because of this, people find it okay to forget me or pick on me.

I'm not great with people, even when I was loud and outgoing. People just found me annoying and mean. Although to my defense, I was never trying to be mean on purpose; I spoke before I processed what I heard. So I changed and I tried to become every piece of what people wanted me to be. I hated myself constantly because I didn't have friends and people didn't like me. It made it worse when my own teachers would turn away when I was being bullied, but that was then.

Now looking back, it was sad, but because of those experiences, it led me to who I am today. Yes, I still have some of these problems internally and sometimes externally, but it doesn't matter what people think of me. I can't keep trying to find myself when I'm almost headed to college. I have to create who I want to be, and who I am comfortable with.

After all this, I still have problems with being an introvert and sometimes I set myself up to fail. I have trouble being sociable especially with my anxiety and depression. I get self-conscious, but I realized that I can't keep holding myself in so other people can feel comfortable, because I'm never going to know how other people feel about the real me. So what I'm asking you for is to please continue to have faith in me and help me be the best I can be because I have never had that. Every teacher sees me for my attendance or grade and though most times those things are the definition of a person, it's not me.

Sincerely,
Frequently Absent

COMMON FRIEND

Dear Teacher,
One of the things I would have liked for my teachers to know is that I'm a shy kid. I never liked presentations or being called on. I'm only not shy around my friends.

The second thing I would have liked for teachers to know is that I don't like to sit with other people I don't know. Just because you put me next to other people doesn't mean we're going to be friends in two days.

The last thing I would have wanted my teachers to know is that I don't like to read books that I don't like. Don't pick out a book that I don't like to read. These are the things I would have liked for my teachers to know.

Sincerely,
Common Friend

Outspoken Soccer Player

Dear Teacher,

There are three things I would like to tell you: I'm very talkative, and I mean no disrespect when I'm being overly talkative; I sometimes just put on my hoodie, without even noticing; and lastly, I love to play soccer. These are the three things I would wish for you to know about me.

First, I wish that you know that I'm a very talkative person. I don't mean to disrespect you. It's just that I can't help not talking to my friends sometimes, especially because I have a lot of friends that I know in class.

Second, I wish you knew that my hoodie goes up without me noticing. I guess you could say that it's a force of habit, but it's very hard to control, especially when I'm in class learning. That is the second thing I would want you to know.

Last of all, I'm a soccer player, and I love the sport. I have been playing for as long as I can remember. I'm happy where it has gotten me today. From playing for the Magics tournament, to playing for the varsity soccer team, I have met so many wonderful people in the soccer community. That is the final thing I wish you knew about me.

These would be the three things I wish you knew about me. I'm a very talkative person; my hoodie just sometimes goes up without me noticing and I'm a soccer player.

Sincerely,
Outspoken Soccer Player

NOT EL

Dear Teacher,

I wish you knew that I'm not an English Learner, and that I should not have been put into EL classes just because all the other Asian kids were. I didn't need the homework to be spoken slowly to me because I'm Asian. I wish you knew that I wasn't a porcelain doll, and I could handle reading and holding thick hardcover books. I could read, so don't try to hand me lower level books all the time. I wish you knew that I wasn't the typical Asian model minority stereotype, and that I couldn't solve whatever math problems whenever I was asked to do so.

I wish you knew that I'm hurt by what the other kids would call me or when they always offer to help me. I wish that they didn't have to ask me, as a second grader, if my parents needed an interpreter during conferences. I also wish my teachers didn't make me sit by all the other Asian children, assuming that we were related or good friends already. I wish my teachers knew that I don't know every other Asian student in the school, or that I could not pronounce every Asian name and word they came across. I wish my teachers didn't have to make a whole day about coloring the Hmong elephant foot design in class because I was the only Hmong student in their class. I wish the teachers knew that I don't know, and I'm not related to the person who made the story cloth they hung in the front of the school. I wish they didn't need to tell me they went to Thailand for a trip and might have met my relatives because they looked like me.

I wish my teachers understood me better and tried to get to know me as a person not a race. I wish my teachers knew.

Sincerely,
Not EL

BARRACUDA BIOLOGIST

Dear Teacher,

I want my teachers to know that I'm into sea creatures, and I like to play soccer. I also enjoy going to my cousin's house when I'm bored. I want to become a biologist and study sea creatures. I also want my teachers to know that I have gone through a lot to get to where I am now, and I can't afford to fail my classes.

The reason I play soccer is because soccer has always been my sport. When I was little, I played soccer with my siblings and cousins. I found soccer fun because it was always competitive between my cousins and I, and it became my favorite sport.

I want to become a biologist to study sea creatures because I'm into sea creatures and learn about the sea world. My favorite sea creature is the barracuda. I'm into barracuda because it's fascinating how fast this creature can be in one burst.

I have gone through a lot to get here. Sometimes I don't understand the homework assignments, which is a challenge for me. I often get distracted by my friends, and sometimes by the girls I have crush on. Overall, I really don't like doing too many homework assignments, but I have to keep pushing myself and doing my assignments anyways because I want to have good grades.

In conclusion, I just want you to know the above about me as I have never told anyone before. Thank you for listening.

Sincerely,
Barracuda Biologist

The Musician

Dear Teacher,

Three things you should know about me is that I'm very quiet, I'm in the marching band, and I'm a little slow.

I'm very quiet in class, in general. I can only be loud around people I have known for a while, but it's hard for me to do presentations, and often time my mind would go blank or get distracted. So, if I would to do any presentation in front of people, it will be difficult for me. I can do it, but I guess I'm just shy and need more practice in the process.

I'm in the marching band, so I like music, not just only band music but all kind of good musics. Music is my life because it helps me to stay focus. I'm a little slow for learning new things at times, so it will take me awhile to get used to new things. I have realized it helps me learn better when I'm listening to music.

I'm shy and quiet in class, but that is how I function. In this language class, I know I have to do stuff in front of the class. I can do all the stuff, like presenting about my project; it's just that I need to get used to it. I'm confident in myself to do more stuff in front of my peers because we're all Hmong.

Like I said before, I'm in the marching band, and I really like music. So, if I tap my feet or tap my fingers in class, that means I'm staying in focus. I find music to be very helpful to me in my learning process. Now you know why I listen to music a lot. I'm aware that I'm a bit of slow at time when it comes to doing things with my peers. Like I said, if I listen to music, it will help me process things through. I don't know why I'm a little slow, but that is how I am. I'm a quiet student, and I tend not to ask a lot of questions. If you ask me a question, I will slowly process the information in my mind and answer you back.

Sincerely,
The Musician

I Don't Want Pity

Dear Teacher,

I'm a 16-year-old who is still growing and learning. I just want you to know a few things about me. I want you to know the person I was before and the person I am now. I don't want any pity. I only want you to hear me and try to understand why I'm the way I am.

Before you became one of my teachers, I was a different student at other schools. I wasn't the best student. I didn't want to learn and often avoided doing anything that would challenge me because I believed I wasn't capable to do it. It's not that I hung out with the wrong people. In fact, I had amazing supportive friends. They always encouraged me to be the best I can be, but somehow, I didn't want to do anything that others encouraged me, or even give it a try. I let every good opportunity passed by because I believed that I wasn't good enough for the opportunities and was ignorant.

During those times I had a lot of family problems that arose. My father married to his third wife and was also still married to my mother. His wife at the time had a son around my age. The son wasn't the best step-brother; he was just an idiot. With him around, there was always rumors in the family. However, I also appreciated some of the good things that he taught me, especially about being a good person. After a year, my step-brother and his mom ran away. I don't know why, and I don't care much anyway.

Today, I'm a better person. Although I have many problems in the past, I try my best to take every opportunity I can. I'm grateful to everyone who has been in my life and is still in my life. Without them, I wouldn't be the person I am today, or I would have given up long ago. I'm thankful for the people who keep pushing me to be the best person of myself. There are hard and difficult moments in life at time, but I'm very happy and appreciate life.

Sincerely,
I Don't Want Pity

SHY GUY

Dear Teacher,
The three things I would like you to know about me is that I'm really shy, I get bored easily, sometime annoyed very easily, and I can't act the way I normally would.

The first thing I want my teacher to know about me is that I'm really shy. I don't like being the center of attention, and I hate the stick name idea thingy. It's too much tension for me. I get a little bit stressed each time you pull them out. The reason I get stressed is because most of the time I don't get what the vowels or things are. Even though I don't know the vowels, I speak Hmong a lot. I speak Hmong at home, and sometimes I speak Hmonglish because we don't have some Hmong words for certain things.

The second thing I would like my teacher to know about me is that I get bored and annoyed easily. You can tell that I'm getting bored from the lesson if I'm playing with my fingers or looking somewhere else. I also get really annoyed by having to repeat myself. If I repeat something more than once then it's no big deal, but if I have to do it three times, I get annoyed by it.

The last thing I want my teacher to know about me is that I can't express my true feelings. I'm am energetic person, and I like to talk; however, I feel very awkward talking to strangers unless I get to know them well. It takes a long time for me to actually feel comfortable being around people. If I have friends, like my old friends in Alaska, I would like our school even more. I could burp around them and feel completely normal because I knew them for a long time and felt really comfortable being around them. I would like to make new friends and talk to some of my peers in class, but I don't know what to do or how to approach them. Most of the time, the way how I make friends is when they started to talk to me first, or the teachers put us together in a group project or something. It helps us connect with one another when we get to do something together as a team. I guess if I get to know people and being comfortable around people, I would talk to them more and even have more fun.

In conclusion, I'm a pretty normal kid doing normal stuff like every other student. As you can tell, I'm really shy in class, and I often get bored or annoyed really easily.

Sincerely,
Shy Guy

You are Perfect Just the Way You are

Dear Teacher,

I wish you knew more about me besides being the quiet kid in most of the classes. Stephen Hawking says, "The quietest people have the loudest minds." I'm one of those quiet people out there. I may seem dull and boring on the outside, but on the inside I'm like a sparkling firework, wild and active. Of course, no one knows my side of the story, and I wish they did. I wish they would put their feet into my shoes and experience what is going on in my life. If I'm lucky enough, my story will be out there, and hopefully someone would read my story and see the world through my eyes. Well, at least I have someone, like you, to share my story with.

I remember when I was younger, I was always active liked a "social butterfly." I wasn't afraid to do things until I grew older. I became more anti-social. I didn't like to socialize unless it was with people I knew well. When I was in fifth grade, things became more stressful for me. I couldn't finish my homework on time, and I was always scolded at because of this. I didn't like it, but I still continued to do the work that was assigned for me. When I reached middle school, I felt invisible, as if no one saw me, or paid any attention to me. I felt like the only people who actually care and saw me as a decent person were my friends, and sometimes few of my teachers if I had done something noticeable. After a while, I started to like the fact of being invisible, but to be honest, I wish I were fully seen and noticed by everyone.

My parents always wish the best for me, hoping that I would get good grades, graduate from college, and get a good job. I try my hardest, so that I could make my parents proud. Sometimes, I also feel like they discourage me, and that make me doubt myself. I started to think negatively towards myself like I'm not good enough for them, or that I'm useless. I normally don't feel sad in my life. I guess a part of me is being sensitive to certain things or issues. I wonder if I could handle criticism.

I guess sometime I just feel like I let everyone down, that I didn't meet anyone's expectations. I wish I'm perfect, and that everyone would just love me. It's just the feeling that if I'm perfect, then no one would judge me. But then, I also realize that no one is perfect in this world. We all have flaws of our own. Everyone makes mistakes, and we learn from those mistakes to grow. The bottom line is, you can't turn into that perfect person of what people expect of you. You don't have to change yourself, you just have to be yourself. You are perfect, just the way you are.

I have learned to accept myself and slowly letting go of the past. Who knows what the future will be? We all just need to take one thing at time. For now, I'm just rolling along with it.

Sincerely,
You are Perfect Just the Way You Are

NUMBER ONE

Dear Teacher,

I know that you probably didn't notice me in some of your classes because there are many other students in it too. Some are loud, and some are smart. I was neither of them, but I was one of those quiet students. There are many times I wished to reach out to you, or other times I hoped you will just find your way to me. So, these are what I wish you knew about me.

My family and I just came to the United States in 2004, and I don't know much English and often struggle in your classes. I don't speak up in class because of the limited English that I know. You probably also noticed that I try really hard to keep up my grades. Maybe you have noticed this before, once one of my subject's grade goes up, my grade in another subject goes down too?

Being the oldest in the family is really stressful because I was the first one to expose to English and learn how to balance between school and responsibility for my siblings. I have to help my siblings with their homework assignments, as well as help my parents with translation. I try my best and continue to do my best to balance everything. I hope you knew about my struggle and help me whatever you can in class.

I wish you knew that I also have some family problems, and sometimes it distracts me from my school work. I know that I should have probably separated the two, but I couldn't because my mother was going to work stressing about my father. He was having affairs with other women and didn't understand the struggle of what my mother was going through, nor what I was facing, as the oldest child. With many days of crying myself to sleep and having head pain, I still managed to smile and come to the school as though nothing happens. Not long after that, I began moving to other schools. Trying to get used to each new system and culture at school, it was hard enough to go through the week. I got used to it because I was ten-year-old by then.

When my family moved from California to Minnesota, everything changed, and I really wished you would understand that everything is very different here. The school system is different, the teachers and subjects and classes are different, and last but not least, the credits required to graduate is different. Beside education and language barrier are not the only thing that my family and I are struggling with. My parents are struggling to find any good paying job. It's easy to understand because they know very little English. By this time, my siblings and I are getting to know our schools and this new school system in Minnesota. I, being the oldest child in the family, has now grown up old enough to drive and care for my family.

As life continues, I want you, as my teacher, to know that I have become wiser, and I'm able to manage more now. I'm doing fine, and I will one day become successful. I have a dream, a goal, and a future to look forward to now. I'm doing well, but again, I really did wish that you had known about my struggles and hardships, especially what I went through and the experiences I had during my childhood. I do hope that you will someday read this letter, and I hope you will see that a little Hmong girl, who used to struggle so much, is now doing fine with big goals that lie ahead of her. Thank you for all the bits of knowledge.

Sincerely,
Number One

LEARNING TO GET BETTER

Dear Teacher,
I would like to learn a lot about my Hmong culture and on how to speak it by the time I graduate from my high school year. I was really nervous when I first saw this class, and I realized I'm not the only one who didn't speak Hmong. It gave me hope that I'm not the only one. I'm somewhat glad I took this class. I know the basic words like "Nyob zoo, kuv lub npe hu ua." I lived with my maternal grandparents most of my life. I'm always really nervous whenever I have to speak Hmong, so I pause a lot,

but I'm always trying to if you try to help me, which you do so I'm glad that you do. The reason why I don't know Hmong is because my mom decided not to teach us when we were still like two-year-old because her side of the family was always saying bad stuff to her and her kids, so she didn't want us hearing any of it. I wanted to learn, but the people I have tried learning Hmong with never really helped. That made me feel like I was embarrassed; therefore, I just never really tried learning it after that.

Now that I'm getting older, I'm finally learning how to be better as a son, man, and student. I was never really the type for school, but now that I have changed. I finally understand how much I have missed out on my culture, school, and life in general. I'm still not very expressive in how I feel personally about anything to be honest. I'm not a good kid, but I know my responsibilities. I make sure I'm still that good kid to my parents. I don't want them knowing of what I used to do because of my depression, or whatever. It's harder for me to even tell them how I feel about myself, or what I want to do with my life. My mom mostly wants to see me do better than anyone else in our family, but at the same it's so hard for me to even keep myself together. I know I'm only a sophomore, but I handle my business myself. No one ever really helps me do anything, but I help a lot because that is just the way I am. This whole year has been everywhere for me and my family; we have had our ups and downs, but in the end, we're always going to be family. Anyways, enough talking about my family.

What motivates me to be who I am and who I want to become in the future is my family and my self-conscious. What drives me to do what I want later in life are business, money, art, investment, stuff like that. I'm also a book worm, so I will read anything that interests me. What brings me down is people who don't appreciate what I do for them or people who doubt me and my self-consciousness. I'm a hesitant person when it comes to really hard choices, but also the easy choices too. Whenever I'm serious with something, I'm like the smartest person in the room. That is how I have always been with my family and other people around. I'm also a guy who fails at a lot of things like tests, talking, making friends, but at the same time, I still try my best. It may not meet other people's expectations, but it will certainly reach mine and only mine because it's my own choices and my choices only.

The choices I made is who I am today. If you choose to have bad addictions, then you chose it. If you choose something that will benefit with your life, then that is your choice to make. Some people I have talked to said it's not easy making choices, but in reality there is always that split second of time where you have time to think of every possibility to make a choice in your life to either do something you will regret or making the best decision of your life. I don't know if you will actually read all of this, but I didn't really have time to think about this, so if you would like to know about my life story of how I am today, you are welcome to ask me. I hope this year goes well for you and your classes. I hope you will continue doing what you love. Like I said, I'm excited and nervous for this year, and it's going to get more challenging as expected so thank you for that!

Sincerely,
Learning to Get Better

Complete Makeover

Dear Teacher,

 I have been going to school in the same district for fifteen years now and will continue to do so until I graduate. This letter is about how I started off my life and show how much I have changed from the start to where I am now. I will gladly share my letter as this will be somewhat nice to get off my chest since I have never really shared the beginning of my life with anyone else beside my family and close friends. If you are willing to read this letter, I will take your hands and show you the start of a life about a quiet Hmong kid who is currently in his sophomore year in high school.

 First off, during my years in elementary school I have always been a quiet, introverted and dumb kid who could never do anything right. Since I never went to any school or place, I was taught only the basics of what my parents could provide. When I was six years old, I was sent to kindergarten immediately to learn. I can tell you it wasn't that great of an experience. The kids were nice to me, but I always felt different compared to them. It wasn't because I was one of the few Asian kids in my class, but it was because I lacked everything they had like socializing or being smart. A flame kindled in me burned, so I decided to change myself. I started to become more outgoing and started to pay more attention in class, so I can match my peers. With every passing school year, I improved little by little, but it wasn't enough. I had quite a number of friends, but my intellect could have been better, and I ended up becoming a C student. I was completely devastated and felt like changing myself was all for nothing, which left me on the verge of tears throughout the rest of the school year. I kept this silence from everyone else. Once sixth grade ended, I swore to myself over the summer I will improve and go beyond my regular expectations of doing above average in school.

 Secondly, I'm not that smart, so almost everyone looked down on me and acted like I had no future in my life from teachers to my friends and even my own parents. My parents would stress out and say there is no hope for me and that I might be able to get into a community college if I try a bit harder and work at a job that pays decently. While they did say these things to me, I still had support from them. Out of my brothers and sisters, I was the smartest, so they depended on me and knew I had potential to grow which was heartwarming. I remembered in elementary school, we did an activity where kids would pick out who would be successful in life by tapping them on the shoulder, and the kids who were going to be tapped had to close their eyes. I was of course peaking since I wanted know who was who, and I got tapped only once because my friend felt a bit bad for me since most people knew I wasn't that smart. I envy those who got A's on their tests and homework while I got stuck with C's and sometimes I would get a "B" if I worked hard enough. Finally, when summer break came around, I had three whole months to improve my brain and become a different person than the one I used to be. This internal thinking would later transform me to become who I am currently.

When I came to middle school as a seventh grader, I felt like a different person. I was so focused and hardworking to the point that I earned a spot in the B honor roll, and when I got home I showed the certificate to my parents and they were ecstatic. They gave me praise and took me to a restaurant to celebrate my achievement; this was nice. I really wondered why they would do all of this over a simple "B" honor roll because it seems like a simple thing to achieve, but nonetheless I enjoyed the moment. I continued my seventh grade year earning more "B" honor rolls and earning praise from both my friends and my parents. Even though I felt nothing from the praise I receive because recently, I had my sight on the "A" honor rolls, but that wouldn't happen until the next school year. Eighth grade was when I completely changed myself; while seventh grade was a change, I was still somewhat the same compared to my elementary self. During eighth grade, I finally achieved A honor rolls because of the efforts I put into studying and believing myself. I was able to go to my middle school honors' night and in front of hundreds of students, their parents and my parents. I received a medal and certificate for my efforts. Everything started going uphill from there on. My parents put their whole faith in me and now I became the person who I am today.

By reading this letter, I would like you to think of me as nothing more, but a student who intends on achieving great things in his future since I don't like being treated as someone special because I hate the spotlight more than your average student. Nonetheless, it was nice to write this letter to someone who is willing to read three whole paragraphs about a person's life and what a person has gone through in order to make a big change for the sake of his future. Because you are going to read this paper, I'm willing to put more effort in working in your class and hope you know I have a passion for learning, especially my native language. Thank you for reading my letter. I hope to meet your expectations in this class.

Sincerely,
Complete Makeover

GRATEFUL FOR AMAZING PEOPLE

Dear Teacher,

Why do I always expect myself to do so much for others and myself? My whole life I thought that I was going to always succeed with the same friends I have been with for years. Having time to do what I love even if I had other things to do. It has now been almost impossible to do anything that I want to do because of how busy I have been with school. I used to never really care about quotes at all. It was never really a motivation or something I believed was true. Now the more I experience new things and get out of my comfort zone, it's like all those quotes coming to life.

I expect myself to do better than others, but when I think about it, it's like I try too hard at being better and fail instead. When I'm nervous I can't focus at all and I start daydreaming and think about other things. Doing better means working harder than others. I will have to work twice harder than everyone. I have never really been the smart one or even the clown of the class. I wanted to focus on being "popular" because I thought it was going to be cool. Then when I did become the top dog somehow. I couldn't really focus in school anymore. I was too into my friends. I soon knew that I had to do both: have friends and succeed at the same time.

Succeeding with friends is difficult if we all have different dreams and wouldn't be there for each other as much anymore. We all will be busy preparing to succeed. I mean they were always by my side and supporting me until things happened with other friends. We all soon started drifting apart. I mean mostly me because I felt like I would be better off without them. Maybe I am? Ever since I stopped being so close to them, I have been lonely, but I haven't gotten distracted from doing my work. I'm the type of person that if someone talks to me, I will just keep talking.

I think that even if someone is busy with life, they could always try to at least find time for what they want to do, so they wouldn't be so worked up. I feel like school now and days gives more and more work. Teachers want to push us to get better, and we can get better, but I'm tired of being tired. If they wanted to give more work, teachers should make things fun. When I was playing football, I thought it was going to be fun. It was fun for a while until my coach stopped putting me in. That is when I really gave up on football, but I had friends who were telling me I should not.

Out of all the people who kept telling me the same things, I had one guy friend who I thought I would never be friends with. He really helped and encouraged me. He was the reason I stayed in sports, making me realize I was worth something. He told me, "it's okay to fall down, but never stay down." That really helped me to pick myself up. I'm glad to have supportive and caring people in my life. I'm glad I picked myself up. I'm grateful for amazing people.

Sincerely,
Grateful for Amazing People

MUCH LOVE

Dear Teacher,
I have been through a lot in life, and I have learned a lot of things on my journey up to now. It has been awhile since I have felt like I don't belong

to a community of people. As an Asian American, I felt like I didn't belong with other people at my school, since most of them were of other races other than Asian. I have had hard times making new friends since first grade when my parents moved us here. I have lived here ever since I was about seven years old, and I didn't know anyone at my school when I first transferred, and it left me hurt. I was that new student who had known no one and had no friends.

One thing about me is that I have been really into cars ever since I was a child. I love the feeling of being in a vehicle that is going fast on the highways or roads. It's a good feeling that has grown on me, especially the rush of adrenaline you get, as you fear crashing or hitting something. It's also the excitement of going at really fast speed on roads, either as the driver or a passenger. That adrenaline rush is a good feeling to me because I feel like I belong in a vehicle that is capable of going faster than an average car. I have been a long-time car enthusiast, and I love Japanese cars. My dad used to own a sports car, and I would always love to ride in the passenger seat with him while he drove us to my cousin's house or to shop at the stores. Sadly, he sold the vehicle to pay for bills and put food on the table. As a child I remember wanting that vehicle that he had and wanting to drive it when I get my license. But I understand why he sold it. Even now I still think about getting my dream car from being successful in the future.

Another thing about me is that I love playing football. It's one of the things I love doing it to help me exercise and destress. I'm a very competitive person, and I would love to play football in the future, maybe even in the NFL. As a child I always loved to play sports, and my interest in football made me enjoy playing it more than any of the other sports I have played before. This past year until now I wanted to join the football team, but I couldn't because I had to stay home to watch my baby sister and wouldn't allow to leave the house much. I love playing football, but my family matters to me more than anything. I would love to be on the football team in this school; it's just that I don't have the time to spare to be at practice, do my homework, take care of my baby sister, and all other stuff in one day. Sometimes being the oldest in my family is a pain, but I understand the responsibilities that I have to take care of my family as my parents both work during the day. It's kind of a let down to me because I want to get better at playing football, but I also don't have the time to practice because of my family.

The last thing about me is that I have been in a relationship for almost two years now, and I'm happy that my girlfriend is with me. The most special person to me in my life is my girlfriend. She gives me motivation, and she supports me the most with anything I want to do. She means everything to me. I plan on marrying her in the future because I feel that she is the right one for me. I love her, and I feel as if I would lose a part of me if I lost her. We have a rough journey, but I feel like I belong with her. We support each other, and I have helped her with her school, and she has helped me with everything happening with me ever since middle school. I met her in middle school, and when I saw her for the first time, I just fell in love with her. I feel like she really is an angel that came from heaven, just to be with me. I don't feel like I'm fully myself without her. She is my other half, and I feel as though I was led down this path just to be with her. She has helped me a lot during middle school and high school, and I just feel as though I can't live without her.

In conclusion, I just really love playing football, Japanese cars, and I just can't live without my girlfriend. I'm a very competitive football player when I try my hardest, and I'm really a car guy when it comes to Japanese Domestic Market (JDM) vehicle. I love my girlfriend with all my heart, and I wouldn't give her up for anything in the world. I'm the luckiest guy in the world to have her. I feel like I wouldn't be myself without these three things in my life, and I'm grateful for what I have in my life, and I wouldn't want it to ever change.

Sincerely,
Much Love

AMAZING JOURNEY

Dear Teacher,

Throughout my life it has been such an amazing journey so far. The life I have been given from my parents are so much more than anyone in the world could ask for. I'm grateful for every little thing my parents have done for me. The hard part of my life is trying to find who I am as a person and what I'm willing to sacrifice to reach the dreams and goals I have thought of.

My parents are truly the best; it's just that they are not understandable with my reasonings and lecture me every time for it. I don't blame them though as I know what life was and is like for them. They have sacrificed so much for our family, so we could have a better life and chance of succeeding and don't have to suffer and live the life they have right now. All my parents want is for us to have a better life than them, so we don't have to worry about how much we can eat or have our kids worry about how other kids have it so much better. My parents are truly amazing, for my dad and mom got married at a young age, and throughout their marriage there has never been a physical fight and rarely yelling. But when they do, it's always easy, and my mom always says, "Never hold grudges as it's always better to be positive and nice." They want to set a good example of how things are going to be better if you just accept one another and live for what really matters.

I have seen my parents work double shifts just so we can have food and have enough money for me to get what I desire. They know how it feels to want something so badly and not have enough for it. I don't want to work double shifts to do that. I know not going to college already makes my parents worry a lot about me, but the thing is that we don't all want to play by the rules. The most successful people don't play by the rules.

For my life, I have learned so much from them; however, as I'm getting older I still don't know what I want to do, or if I even want to attend college. I know you will be reading this and feel some type of way towards me, but trust me that I do have my reasonings and as to why I'm willing to do what I'm going to do.

I'm prepared for all the hate, but also prepared to be me and do what I think is right for me. I hope my parents live long enough to see me succeed because they are getting old and sick. My uncle (dad's brother) just recently passed, and it was so sad because it has me thinking we really don't know when we will leave this world but to hope for the best.

The thing I do best is overthink and it's killing me. I stress everyday about every little thing going on in my life. I know I should not worry too much or I will be sick too, but I can't help it. I like to play football or games, just to get lost in the world of questioning myself every second of my life. No one understands me truly, but it's what it's since everyone is different.

Football season starts a week before school started, and I was prepared to give it all I got. I know I'm undersized to play the sport, but my love for it's too much to give up. I have stressed over my size, but the Football coach has been nice to me and showed me love. He talks to me and smiles every time which brightens up my day without him knowing.

I'm a starter on defense even though I wasn't expecting myself on defense I think it was for the better knowing my mom doesn't want me to get injured, as offense gets injured the most.

School wise I have always been a below average kid, not so good, but not bad enough to not pass my classes. My elementary and middle school years were the worst. I struggled with everything and was barely passing at times. My freshman year was the best year for me as I was able to get 6 A's and 1 B; therefore, I felt so proud of myself and knew what I can really achieve. Not going to lie, but as a kid I was naughty, so I can see why I had bad grades since I also slacked a lot and procrastinated. I have always been quiet in class though because every time I speak I feel so ignored when the teachers don't even want to listen to me, and their body language says it all.

Throughout my life I have been isolated from my family, for I'm always alone with no one to talk to. All my siblings are much older so I can see why, but I just don't get along with anyone of them. My siblings and I don't talk much and when we do, it's always do this or that, or short talks.

My life now is where I think it should be at. I'm still on my two feet in my own shoes doing my own things. For my future I just pray everything works out the way I see it, but for that to happen it starts with me changing my laziness and procrastination to self-discipline. I believe that self-discipline is the key to success as you are willing to do the things needed to get where you want to be. Your dreams are never handed to you and I feel like in this society, Hmong people are the least successful as they don't have enough of a certain thing and just give up on their dreams or goals completely, which is not fine because everyone has a chance at life and should strive for the best. Like you said, "Always set for the best, so when you do a little worse you still did good." This will always be with me from now on and with my mindset, thanks teacher. Well this completes my life so far so let us see what the future holds.

Sincerely,
Amazing Journey

INTRODUCTED STORYWRITER

Dear Teacher,
There are not many things that you know about me that I would like for you to understand. As a student, I wish you knew that I'm very shy, like to learn about history, and write stories.

I mostly prefer to keep to myself and stay quiet during class. Thinking helps me relax when I'm having a bad day, or something is annoying me. I generally talk only when I need to talk. I don't like doing presentations because I can't speak well in front of a large audience. I have a troubling time making new friends, so most of my friends are ones that I have known for quite a while. Even during times of socialization, I prefer to keep to myself. I like to occupy myself by watching a show, reading something, or listening to music. I would say that I have an introverted personality.

My favorite subject is history for a few reasons. The first reason why I prefer history over other subjects is because I have a drive to learn about it. I always find history more interesting to learn over other subjects. To me, history is an endless source of information with many different interpretations.

The second reason why I like history is because the cultures of each group of people is very different and interesting to learn. People's cultures may develop differently based on their geography and their surroundings, such as languages that have words with no equivalent to another language. The way people's cultures and traditions develop is very interesting to me.

The third reason why I like history is to learn about the history of my people. Hmong history is not often written into documents. The only way to learn about the history of my people is by asking the elders, who usually don't speak English. This is one of the main reasons why I took Hmong class. For me, history is such an interesting and ever-expanding subject. There are always new things to learn, and it can always change.

The last thing that I would like for you to know is that I like to write stories. Although I'm not a very good essay writer, I really like to write stories. I prefer to write stories on my own time and without a grade to judge it. I feel when I write a story for an assignment, it limits my imagination for the story. I get inspiration from other stories or events in the past. Some of my favorite things to write are short stories. Short stories don't require a long investment of time and energy and only take me a few hours to write. Although short stories are my favorite to write, I will occasionally write a longer story. So far, I have only written two books. I don't share my longer stories with anyone, except my family because I think the stories are kind of embarrassing. Writing expands my imagination and relaxes my mind.

To conclude, I'm very shy, like to learn about history, and write stories. As my teacher, you may not have understood why I do some of these things. Now that you have read this, I hope these explanations help you know a little more about me.

Sincerely,
Introverted Storywriter

What If

Dear Teacher,

How are you doing today? Listening to all your stories about your life and the struggle you went throughout your journey really inspire me to never give up and to keep going no matter how long it takes to succeed or be happy. You can't change who you were born to be, but you can change who you can end up being. Sometimes your stories make me sad and emotional or all types of feeling, but now you are in a place where you are happy. In this letter I will be sharing three things about me. Thank you for giving me this chance to share about me because I don't think I have told anyone this much about myself.

First of all, I'm actually really similar to you as a student. I was that shy student who almost never raised her hand. I would get all A's and A-'s- and people would think I'm so smart and all that. But in reality, it's mostly because I'm not a really good communicator and tend to not have as much friends, so I just concentrate on work and be independent. I'm also really scared of having people judge me, so I just stay quiet. On top of that, I have a soft and quiet voice, so when I share out my answers and the teachers can't hear me, they ask me to repeat it and then I start to lose confident. Even when I know the answer to a question or have an idea about something, I just don't want to say it. I'm not sure what the reason is, but I just have this thought or feeling in my head telling me not to raise my hand. I think now, I'm getting more confident about myself and I'm not as shy as I used to be. I'm starting to raise my hand more, especially in Math. When I get an answer right I have a tendency to get really happy and proud of myself.

Secondly, growing up, my siblings and I were scared of my dad. Not because he abuses us or verbally yell at us, but because of the tone in his voice. He has a loud voice and his tone just really scares me as a kid. Even now, sometimes I would be scared of him. So, when I want to ask to hang out with a friend or something, I would always ask my mom because I'm scared of asking my dad because he would refuse. I never really get to hang out with my friends and such because I would be afraid to ask my parents. Even if it's worth a try because they might let me, I still couldn't do it. So once, when my friend asks me if I could go to her birthday party, I said I would ask my parents, but I actually didn't because the answer would obviously be "No", and then I just tell her I can't go. I think that is one of the reasons why I don't have a really close friend or best friend that I'm genuinely comfortable enough to tell all my secrets to. I have friends, but we're not close enough to comfortably talk to each other. Sometimes, we wouldn't even know what to talk about so we just sit there awkwardly. For the first time last year, I actually gathered up my courage to ask my mom if I could go to a friend's house after school. She said, "Yes", and I was so excited, but I came home around 9 almost 10 and she said she was so worried, so I'm not sure she will let me go again.

The third thing is that I'm scared I might not be able to meet my parent's expectations. Just like almost every other Asian parents, they want me to be a doctor or lawyer or get jobs that pays a lot of money. On the other hand, I just feel like I wouldn't be able to do it, although I'm thinking about doing something in the medical field. As of now, I really don't have an idea of what I will do in the future. I'm just not prepared for anything and I don't know how I will start my life after I graduate from high school. I'm scared and nervous. Just imagining how college life will be like and finding what my passion is, which I don't know because I don't know what I like to do, is nerve-racking. My older sister and parents would often ask me what I want to do in the future and I just say I don't know. Then they would ask, "What do you like to do?" or "What classes do you like?" and I just don't know because I like different things in each class. There are so many things we do in each class and some I like, while others not so much. So, I truly wish to find my passion and what I would like to do in the future.

Another thing I'm struggling with is my parent's broken English. I mean I'm fine with them talking with broken English, but they have a hard time understanding things and often, I don't know how to explain to them. Like, what if I don't pass an exam, or I don't have enough money. I would let them down and they would just question me. I honestly have so many "what if" questions that I'm worried about. I just hope that by the end of high school I will have some knowledge or expectations of the future would be like.

Sincerely,
What If

NOT SO CONFIDENT

Dear Teacher,

I want you to know that I'm really not a quiet kid. I mean I'm in class, and that is because I'm shy and scared to make some kind of interaction with people who I don't know. If you get know me, I'm really loud, and I talk so much that you might want to slap me to be quiet. I love talking to people, more like nice and kind people, or people I know. But I'm just scared to open up to people because I don't want it to be awkward, and I don't know if they would like me or not. I'm very insecure about myself and often worry about every little thing I do. I don't know exactly why, but I just do.

I'm also new here to this school. I just wish I can make more friends, but it's hard because some people think they are too cool for you, or they don't need any more friends since they already have a group to themselves, or they are just two faced. I do have a few friends here, and I barely ever see them. The very first week of school, I was so scared that my heart felt like it was going to burst open any second. Thankfully it didn't. I was so lost and didn't know where I was going, and I went into the wrong classroom. There was this guy who helped me to find my classroom on the other side of the school. He was late for his class, and I felt bad. He was a link crew member and we became friends now.

I'm scared to talk because I don't really know how to start a conversation. I mean I do, but I just don't know how to make it not to be awkward in the beginning of the conversation. There is this one guy who has been on my mind lately, but I'm not sure if he feels the same way about me. We're friends, I guess you could say, but we don't really talk. I try to say "Hi" to him sometimes whenever I get the chance to see him, but my confidence goes down and I just walk away and see if he notices me. This one time he came into my classroom and all of the sudden my heart just went crazy. It was beating so fast and I could feel my face getting hotter by the second. I was going to try to start a conversation with him, but he ran out of the classroom, so I never got the chance to.

Something that brings me down is having two faced friends. I once had these friends who I thought were so kind, and I thought they also saw me as a good friend too. I soon found out that they were talking about me behind my back and pretending to like me - which I don't get it. Why would you do that to a person who treated you so good and was always there for you when you were down and always had your back and helped you? It's just something I will never understand honestly. I guess that is a reason why I can't open up to people easily.

When I get older, I want to travel with my sisters. My sisters would always tell me to enjoy life and appreciate the moment when I'm still young. My dream is to go visit the Bahamas someday. It seems like a beautiful place, and I just love oceans and beaches. There is this one beach that has pink sand, and it's located in Harbor Island. Traveling to new places would motivate me to stay positive. There are so many things out in the world to explore and do. My sisters often tell me that, "You don't want to stay in the same place forever." I appreciate my sisters so much because I learned so much from them, and they are always there for me and giving me advice. They basically raised me because my mom wasn't home that much due to her work schedule from 3pm to 3am.

I love my family so much, but I feel like we have been broken lately. It's not the same anymore as how it used to be five years ago. I barely see my family members, and I should spend more time with them and appreciate them more. I wish I would have gotten to known them more because I didn't really know how to talk to older people. I want to talk to them, but I'm afraid they would always see me as a kid. I guess I just wanted to be myself, and at the same time I don't want them to judge me like I'm just a kid. I just wish I'm close to my family because no matter what, they are still my family. I guess we're all just busy so busy with our life.

A goal of mine is to be a model or an actor, or even both. What pulling me down from chasing this dream is that I don't know if I will be a good model or actor. Being a famous actor in those popular movies is very hard to get in because you have to do exactly what the director wants, or some people will always be better than you.

I think something I need to improve on is my confidence. I have always just let people say what they want about me, or take advantage of me. I just don't have the confidence to confront people and ask why they said such things about me.

I just wish my teachers knew that I'm trying to improve on myself because I honestly don't know anything about myself anymore. I just feel so lost in this big world. As a child growing up, I was so scared to grow up and being alone or feeling lonely. But now it has been really lonely lately, and I'm just scared because I'm just not used to it. I feel like I lost so many people in life, and I can't do anything about it. At the end of the day, I only have my own back. I mean I do have supportive friends that help me, but all that they can really do is just telling me that it's going to be alright. It's my problem, so I have to fight through it.

Quotes are actually another thing that motivates me through life. A few of my favorite quotes are, "If you want a rainbow, you will have to go through the rain." I got this quote from, "The Fault in Our Stars." I really loved that movie because it's just very beautiful. And another quote I love is from Thirteen Reasons Why, and it says, "Sometimes you just have to go on with life because sometimes you can't move on." Reading quotes are just my favorite things to do. It's just something that I can relate to and find peace in it. Another thing that is very helpful when I'm sad is listening to music. It's just so soothing and calming, and I love listening to the lyrics and trying to understand the meaning of it, or how it relates to me. A few of my favorite songs are Neurosis - Oliver Riot, Long Sun - Jez Dior, Lights and Camera - Yuna, Sleepless - G-eazy, and RUDE - Eternal Youth.

It may seem like I'm always sad, but I'm really not. I'm a pretty happy kid. I love my life, but just like a normal person, I have a few things that just get in my way. The year 2018 has made me have a new perspective to life. I'm just scared to grow up because I don't know what I'm doing. I feel so lost. I don't know how to call and make appointments and do taxes. It's just like where do I start. Hopefully, I will have that figured out soon later these years. One last thing you should know about me is that I don't really know much about my language and my culture. One of my goals is to learn how to speak Hmong fluently and be educated about my own culture.

Sincerely,
Not So Confident

LIVING UP TO HIGH STANDARDS

Dear Teacher,
As a ninth grade student, I would like you to know that I really like how diverse this school is. It's nice to know that I'm not the only Hmong student in this grade because I see Hmong students everywhere. I have a cousin who lives in North Carolina, and she is the only Asian person in her grade. She says she has only seen only one other Asian person in that school. I like how there are teachers who make the students laugh and make learning fun and enjoyable. Another thing I like is how we're treated equal in class.

I would like you to know a couple things about me, and these things are very personal or mean a lot to me. First, I want to say that I'm not the best student, as I tend to get myself in trouble at school and at home. I'm not the best learner, to me this means that it takes longer for me to learn. Although I take all these HP and AP classes, I struggle with the subjects and try to work hard to catch up with everyone, as it seems like they have already known everything right away. I know that I could just drop-out of the class, but it's embarrassing to be that person who dropped out. Therefore, I have just gotten so used to it, so it's normal now. At home I feel the same. I have the highest standards out of my whole family. They don't understand that I work three times harder than everyone else while others are just hanging out with their friends or take naps. I know that my life is not as hard as some people who are dealing with real world issues, but I have ever dealt with anything as serious, so my problems are pretty big to me.

Another thing I want to tell you is that I have no idea what I want to do with my life. I don't know who I want to be when I grow up. I hope that you can be the teacher to guide me who I want to be. I know that this wasn't as long as my other paragraphs, but I don't really have anything else to say at the moment. So, I thank you for taking the time to read my letter.

Sincerely,
Living Up to High Standards

ALMOST LOST MY LANGUAGE

Dear Teacher,

Before ninth grade, I went to a Hmong charter school. Teachers over there are the best, and they care about the students. Many years ago, I went to another Hmong charter school where my dad worked. My father worked as a Hmong teacher and usually when I come into his classroom in the morning, he would make me learn my Hmong vowels and consonants. I find it so miserable. During school when my classroom peers come into his Hmong class, he expected me to be the top which I didn't like it at all, and I felt embarrassed.

Over the years, my father worked as the bus transportation coordinator who answered phone calls from parents. During this time period, I lost my fluency in speaking Hmong and started to speak more English at home. It was hard for me to talk to my grandpa. I honestly feel funny and frustrated trying to speak Hmong to the elders. There was this time where I was home alone with my grandpa and then there was this White woman who knocked on our door. My grandpa opened the door and the lady told him that they are asking for a donation and see if he wanted to donate money. She also asked questions. I came over to see what is going on and my grandpa stood there waiting for me to speak. We started talking and my grandpa asked me what she say to me, and I was struggling translating it in Hmong for him to understand. I started to get frustrated and guessed the translation. That is one of the reasons why I decided to come to Hmong class.

One thing I did over the summer is when I went to a Hmong Alliance Church camp called H.L.U.B. Conference. Early morning around 4am, youth members came to church. The coach bus picked us up and drove all the way to Illinois. The H.L.U.B. Conference took place at Wheaton College in Illinois, which is a Christian college. It was a beautiful place. We went to our dorms and unpacked our things. All other Hmong Alliance Church youths came to the camp from all around the U.S. It was amazing meeting other Christian teenagers from a different state. I went to a workshop called "Obey Your Parents." It was taught by Mr. Lee from PCSH. Wow, he was awesome!

Sincerely,
Almost Lost My Language

Very Thankful

Dear Teacher,

All of my teachers have played big roles in my life, and they will play even bigger roles for me in high school, but what I wish you know is that I'm thankful for you dealing with the group of kids that we are. Not just us, but everyone else also. In a world that is quickly changing, all I see are worse and worse kids. So, I'm thankful you stuck around to teach us and help us learn. If I had been in your shoes, I would have given up on the job. I praise you for that.

I also want you to know that you are not the only one who may be tired of disrespectful kids. Kids who wouldn't listen, cause a commotion, or just be plain annoying or do downright dumb things. Maybe it's because I take my education seriously? Tej zaum yog vim tias kuv nyiam kawm ntawv. Maybe it was because I just wanted to get things over with, and when they hold the class back by being rude made it hard to do so?

Whatever the reason, you are not the only one struggling. Teachers have it hard. I'm inspired by you guys. *Thaum peb qw, tsis mloog lus, thiab tsis khes txog kev kawm ntawv, nej tseem rov tuaj thiab. Nej zoo tshaj plaws.*

The last thing I wish my teachers knew was how bored I am. Bored of school. School is too easy. Maybe I should have skipped a grade, or I should have just played around more? I just wish you guys would have taken it upon yourself to diversify the classes, and make some students take it beyond. I felt like I'm being held back, but that is just me being selfish. Looking back, you guys have done a lot for me. Sure, the days can be boring. Classmates are annoying, but I really want to thank you guys. I hope other students realize how much you are trying to do for them.

Sincerely,
Very Thankful

MUST DO IT

Dear Teacher,
I would like you to know that I like this class very much. I think it helps me to become a better person in my culture and heritage. I hope that I could learn how to speak, read and write in Hmong better than I already do. I want to be able to speak to my grandparents without hesitating to say a word. There are a lot of things I want to be able to do with my language. I hope that I could speak as good as a native speaker fresh from Laos. And I know that it will take much perseverance and determination

in order to reach my goal of becoming a more advanced native speaker.

Now on the topic of me. I'm the second oldest of my siblings and the oldest son. I'm the tallest of my family, just an inch taller than my dad. I had a sister who passed away when I was younger. My sister also had your class. She is just a year older than me.

I want to be successful in life with a Master's degree in computer engineering. I love to play fighting with my little brother, even though sometimes I make him cry because I go to hard. I always comfort him after hitting so hard. One of my biggest inspirations is my dad because he was a top student in his high school days, and I set a goal to achieve just as much as my dad did, or even more. My mom is also my inspiration because she was also a top student, never being distracted for what was right.

Mostly every summer I have to go help my grandparents at their farm for about two months. Even though I don't want to, I'm forced to do it, so I bear it. I also go to the farmers markets with my grandparents, so I can help them sell their vegetables and those beautiful flowers that they cut from the farm to sell at the market. Maybe when I'm getting older, I will be willing to go help them more often, but as of right now I'm still just a kid, so going to help them all the time is not my ideal summer.

I can really achieve something if I put my mind and heart into it. I'm a really bad procrastinator, and I like to do things last minute. However, when it's last minute, I often get panic and rushed through it, and it doesn't really turn out as expected. But I'm trying to change my laziness in procrastinating because it will be very bad for me now and in the future when I'm in college.

One of my favorite things to do is drawing. I like to draw many things, and I mostly draw cartoonish characters. I can also draw realistic too, but it just takes a little more time. My other hobbies are relaxing even though that is barely a hobby, it's just something I like to do. I have done a variety of sports before, those including soccer, football, and swimming. I participated in soccer and swimming for my high school, and it was pretty challenging.

But all things aside, I know it will be a hard and tiring road of getting to college and succeeding in it, especially to get my Master's degree. I know there will be obstacles in the way, some that may seem impossible to break through, but I know nothing is impossible even the word itself tells you: "I-am-possible." I have to learn to overcome those obstacles and high school will help me. High school is like the pre-test compared to college which is the final exam. I would like to think that optimism is the best in some situations, for I always want to be a kind person with no cons, but I know that is impossible, and this one is for real. Not everyone is perfect, and neither am I, as I have many flaws as discussed in sections above. I can always fix those flaws. Well, we talked about everything and I will, I know, pass college with flying colors.

Sincerely,
Must Do It

STRESS FREE

Dear Teacher,
I want you to know that I'm a very mature student. I may not know everything, but I do know a lot about real life because I have experienced it from a poor family. My family is doing fine now, so that is out of the way. I have been through a lot because of the many unfortunate things that

happened to my family. So, I learned a lot when I was a child, more than I feel I was supposed to.

I also want you to know I'm a very cheerful student. I use my laughter to cope with everything because no one will understand me on the inside. I started to notice that no one can understand me, unless they have gone through my life, or been in my shoes. So, that is why I laugh so much. I believe that laughter can cure any sadness because everyone loves to laugh, and it gives them butterflies. Laughter lets me be myself sometimes.

In conclusion, I want you to know I'm a very observant person. I don't know why, but I just am. I can tell when someone is having a hard time with school, life, family etc.... It's something I developed from being a very quiet person, and I learned or aware of other people's shoes that they might be going through something in life like what I had. I also like being relied on by others because I love the feeling of someone is needing me, since I really love helping others. If someone needs help, it's really hard for me to say no because I would feel too bad, and I would want to help them. I'm also a very relaxed person because I really don't think there is a reason people need to stress. Stress just causes a burden, and I don't need that in my life.

Sincerely,
Stress Free

ALMOST LOST MY HMONG

Dear Teacher,

My family decided that our old neighborhood wasn't safe for us anymore and that it was too dangerous to walk around, so they decided that we should buy a house in this area. This new house is located in between two suburban districts. The house is beautiful, big enough for a family of eight, and it has room for everyone. I didn't want to leave my old city because I was leaving so many opportunities behind, and I was leaving some that people I cared a lot, especially my friends and former teachers. I didn't want leave them.

Over the summer, we moved to our new family house nears this school area. When I first came to the main entrance doors of this school, I didn't know what to expect. On the first day of school, I had a tour and met with my teachers. I remembered the first day of school, I wanted to go home so bad because I felt like I didn't belong here. I missed my old friends and teachers. It got to the point that I just cried because I didn't feel like I belong in this place, or just being myself like I used to be with people I know. I kept telling myself everyday that everything is going to be alright.

I'm a Hmong daughter and am the oldest child in my family. I have five younger siblings whom I am watching over and take care of when my parents are at work. My dad always wanted me to learn the tradition ways of a Hmong daughter should be, like learning how to cook for the family and help raise the younger siblings. It's pretty much a Hmong family's value that we all contribute together in order to live stable.

Growing up wasn't easy for me because I didn't know English that well. I was raised by both of my grandparents at home when my parents were busy at work. My grandparents only spoke Hmong to me, but once we moved away, my parents started to speak more English to me. They finally enrolled me to a public elementary school in order to improve my English-speaking skills. Over the years as I started to speak more and more English and my Hmong began to fade away to the point when I speak in Hmong, it would sound funny to the elders' ears or the ears of my friends who spoke Hmong fluently. I was made fun of because I didn't understand Hmong anymore, or I couldn't speak it as fluently as the others who did. It frustrated me because they didn't know how it felt to lose your own native language, that is a part of your identity. Even so, people who I knew wouldn't correct me on how I said things, or tell me what this meant in Hmong; instead they would only just leave me looking helpless. The only person who didn't judge me is my grandmother who understood why my Hmong had faded, and that I could only speak a few words of Hmong now.

Sincerely,
Almost Lost My Hmong

BLANK FACE WHO IS NOT WHAT YOU THINK

Dear Teacher,
Hearing that this letter gives me an opportunity to share anything that I wished my teachers know about me, gives me hope. I would like to tell you something I have never informed to all of my past teachers, and such topics that I never had the guts to talk to friends and family members

about. I will try to make this letter less personal as possible since I find it foreign for people to worry about me and give me the entirety of their attention.

Based on the previous sentence, it might give you a clue that I don't truly understand and don't know how to handle emotions and feelings, but I do laugh, smile, and cry for simple reasons. I'm not a 100% stoic or emotionless person; in fact, I can remember the last time I laughed, smiled, and cried. I also don't want you to come to a conclusion that my childhood traumatized me or anything bad about my past.

To get to the point, one example is that I don't relate to when someone says they feel euphoric when they find true love, which is not something surprising, but I would feel happy for them as romantic feelings are something I just side eyed for a long time. Maybe it's the fact that the last time I developed a serious crush was when I was in fifth grade, or that I know that I'm not someone capable of expressing the same amount of love back? Whenever my friends felt down or needed support and help, they would tell me that I don't answer with "enough" love and care. As a result, it made me angry because I felt like I was obligated to exceed my limits of emotions and feelings, and those that don't exist within myself just to show that I was understanding of what they were going through.

It's not just the positive emotions and feelings, but it's also negatives ones. Emotions that keep me bound from doing anything take over my mind leaving no space for thinking, those that over-breached my limits of living, or makes me feel empty when I have everything. I always feel extremely sad and unworthy, but I don't self-diagnose myself as a person falling into depression because I'm convinced it's driven from my state of isolation and loneliness. This letter is to give you a notice that whenever I'm showing a blank face when news gets told, I'm not radiating uninterest or boredom, but I just tend to not show emotions physically in an environment, and with people that I'm not familiar with.

Everything is kept within myself which is like a private rant account that someone goes on to shoot off their opinions and emotions to keep calm and satisfy themselves, but sometimes I tell it to a friend or two, not all. Thanks for listening.

Sincerely,
Blank Face Who is Not What You Think

⧉ ⧉ ⧉ ⧉ ⧉ ⧉ ⧉ ⧉ ⧉ ⧉ ⧉ ⧉ ⧉ ⧉ ⧉

PASSIONATE LEARNER

Dear Teacher,

The intent of this assignment is to introduce myself and share three things about me. First, I'm the first generation of Hmong-American. Secondly, I'm a Hmong-Christian, and third, I'm a passionate learner.

As mentioned above, my ethnicity is Hmong. I have two sisters, two brothers and we all live with my parents and my grandmother, who is 84 years old. I was born at a local hospital. Then, my family moved to Rochester, Minnesota, when I was one-year-old. My family lived in Rochester for some time then we moved to this area.

The second fact about me is that I'm a Hmong Christian. My family and I attend First Hmong Assembly of God Church, a Hmong church located in the east-side of Saint Paul, Minnesota.

The third fact about me is that I'm a passionate learner. My father always reminds my siblings and me, "Education is the key to success in this today's world." I've committed to myself that I will succeed in school and become a Dentist in the future.

I'm excited to be a learner in the Math and Science Program here. I'm grateful for the opportunity for me to be part of the learning process.

Sincerely,
Passionate Learner

MOTIVATED HMONG

Dear Teacher,

What I want you to know about me as a Hmong student is that most people don't know how to say my name, but it's fine. I'm able to say it, but I know it's hard to pronounce.

I'm a person who really dislikes hypocrites and people who always believe they are right. I just think that way they act is really mean and selfish, and they show no respect. I also don't really like liars either.

I'm also a person who shows respect a lot. I think that everybody should be treated with respect. I don't think that a person would be very kind, if no respect is shown by them. Respect is something that I'm really serious about.

I don't like to be with people who are troublemakers, and violent people either. They seem to be failing at life, so I don't really hang out with them. I think if I'm around positive people, I will be more successful for my family and myself.

Sincerely,
Motivated Hmong

FINDING LOVE

Dear Teacher,

I wish you knew how it feels to try your best and still not be enough. It's a bit hard when you have pressure all weighed onto your shoulders. I wish you knew my pace is slower, even slower than regular students. I'm not an A honor roll student, barely a B honor roll student. I only get it here and there. No one ever seems to notice me.

She is struggling to breath and struggling to seize potential in herself. She is trying to make an effort to prove to her family and friends she can do anything. That she can go on proving and achieving her dreams. She just wants to be loved and cherished by her loved ones. Her teachers may think she is just always wondering off in her thoughts. She is strangled in her thoughts, drowned with many challenges ahead of her.

I should have told you how scared I'm about my future. Even the first day of school, it doesn't matter what grade. I start to panic once the teacher's eyes are on me and I already feel the negative thoughts they may be thinking about me. I'm not saying they are, but just as a first impression. As a student, I try to make the best first impression just like when you try to make a first impression when applying for a job. As a student, we try to impress our professors, so that they can be able to tell our family and friends that we're just as great. But I struggle to find myself, sometimes when I can't get the love from family. I often run off outside the box to feel loved, even when we're too young to know anything about love. So, that is what I did. I went somewhere else other than family to feel like I'm needed, to be comforted and especially to feel loved. Even more, even when I went outside the box, I still wasn't getting anything from anyone else. Maybe I actually didn't need love from outside the box, but I just needed my family to support and be willingly to listen to me?

I canceled a few great offers to make the family happy; I once let my only chance to success go. I started to do everything wrong, no matter what happened in the family house, I did everything wrong. Then that was the day when I started to go downhill and even my patience started to be empty. My patience level downgraded and my anger started to increase. Then, from there I stopped believing in me. I hope that you will listen to my letter without judgement.

Sincerely,
Finding Love

FASHION MODEL

Dear Teacher,

I wish you knew the little things about me and my life. Lately I have been falling into depression and been stressing. Ever since school came, long it has been a rocky road. Night after night I would have homework and it fills up my weekend, so I wouldn't have time to spend with my family. In my AP U.S. History class, I feel like I don't even belong in there. I lose a little bit of motivation day-by-day, but I tell myself to keep going. At home my parents' relationship has started to become a little rocky, but it has been patched up again. I have become afraid when my parents argue and I can't do anything, but be there for my siblings.

I'm not just your silent, non-talkative student, but I'm someone who has huge thoughts constantly roaming my mind. I like speaking my thoughts about politics and engaging in the problems of today's society. I like doing poetry as well. When I write poems, I create an image inside my head of what I want to write down. If I'm thinking about an ocean, I will write about how deep and blue the ocean is.

I picked up a new hobby and it's modeling! Who would have known someone like me would do modeling? My cousin paved me a way to becoming a model by letting me help her with photography. Ever since I have started modeling I have never felt so comfortable in my own skin, and I have never felt this much confidence in a while. I want to pursue my modeling career, but I don't know when and how. Hopefully by the time I turn sixteen I can start earning money from having a job.

These are just a few updates about my life. I hope one day I will look back and see how far I have come and overcame when I read this letter again next year. These are just a few things I wished you knew about me, my teacher.

Sincerely,
Fashion Model

TRANSFORMED AMBIVERT

Dear Teacher,
During elementary school, middle school and my freshman year of high school, I was an introvert. I was a quiet kid who didn't like to talk a lot because I was shy and embarrassed. In elementary school, I had a feeling that some of the teachers didn't like me. I remembered when a teacher avoided my question which made me doubt myself. When middle school

came around, I was still really shy. I never liked presenting because my biggest fear was messing up in front of everyone. I had many things to say, but didn't have enough courage to speak up. That was my school life up until freshman year of high school.

After freshman year, I became more comfortable talking in front of the class, presenting, and asking questions. I stopped caring about what others thought of me because I didn't know them, and they didn't know me. Although sometimes I can get nervous when presenting even to this day, I do my best at all times. I would now consider myself as an ambivert. Today I'm a senior doing my best to stay on track to graduate. I hope to pass all my classes with decent grades.

When high school is over I plan to go to college. I'm working for my Master's degree, but I'm not sure what major yet. I want to have a future where I don't have to worry about money, and to be able to support my parents. They have done and sacrificed a lot for my siblings and me. My goal is to do the same for them when I'm older. I know I will have many obstacles ahead in life after high school is over, and I will do my best to get through them, so I can reach my goal of supporting a family of my own and my parents.

Sincerely,
Transformed Ambivert

Your Super Positive Student

Dear Teacher,

I wish you knew that a while ago my grandpa had passed away due to cancer. I don't know why he had it and why it had to be him, but he did many great things for our family and many other Hmong families too. My grandpa fought in the Secret War. He nearly died then because soldiers were near the area to attack and my grandpa had to quickly go into the river and hold his breath. The soldiers had looked around for a long time and my grandpa had almost died due to not having any more oxygen, but thankfully he didn't. I wouldn't be here today if it wasn't for him and I'm still amazed at what he did.

Whenever I feel down, I wish my grandpa was there next to me. I wish I could talk to him and ask him questions because I would love to get to know him better. I want to know what he did during his free time and how he and my grandma met. I want to know what he taught my dad and how he was like when he was my age. I hope I become someone as strong as he was and see him again one day.

Teacher, I wish you knew that at times I feel strong hatred towards how people around me act like. Social media is definitely something that gets to me. It's not the app itself, but what people post on there. It gets very unhealthy and people don't even see that anymore because they think it's all just normal. All I ever see is negativity and because of that, I don't go on it as much anymore because it wastes my time and doesn't help me become a better person. I wish that people would see that the world, mainly the people in it, as not always as bad as they think it is though, because there is more out there than they know! There are many good things that you can do instead of going on social media only to see and posts about all of the negative things going on in life. Why not post what you did with your family that day or post about something you finally accomplished? Every day I come to school and hear people talk about how they hate this or that. It's always about another person or even themselves. I feel that they are very unappreciative of the life they live in. They like to look at the things that have been bringing them down, but you should always try to make you and your world a better place. Look at the good and leave the bad behind.

The last thing I would like to mention is that I find it important to empower others. You will never really know what someone is going through. Although at times I feel down, I still try my best to bring others up because I know that that is what I would want to feel like: better and happy. It's not just about making others feel better though, but it's also about encouraging others to try their best at what they love to do. Whatever makes them happy, encourage them to keep going at it because it will lead them to many opportunities and maybe even a greater life. Why would you ever want anyone to feel or be worse than they already might be? I'm a believer in the saying "treat others how you would like to be treated" I mean, it's true, is it not? I treat others well because that is how I would like to be treated. If you ever treat someone badly, why is that? You wouldn't want to be treated badly either. What goes around will come around, bad and good. Thank you for reading my mind.

Sincerely,
Your Super Positive Student

GIFTED & LONELY

Dear Teacher,

Honestly when you first gave out this assignment I was very skeptical if you actually wanted to know who I was. Afterall I had gotten assignments like this before and teachers normally just blow it off. It's always the same cycle, I write something that actually matters to me, but they just grade it, and never talk to me again. Although you were different, you showed me that you actually cared. You didn't just care about me, you cared about every single student, just like our old letters. You saved each one, you read each one several times a year, so that is why I'm going to write my truth because now I know you are definitely willing to listen.

When I was is third grade, I had just moved into town, and really hated it. First things first, this may sound very insensitive, but I could tell as a kid my education wasn't growing. I had just come from a richer district where we had more of an advanced learning, so when I moved and started a new elementary school, I really did think how dumb these kids actually are. I didn't like the fact that I had to relearn things I had already learned how to do in second grade. For example, I remember vividly I learned how to multiply in second grade and these kids could barely do addition, it was annoying to see myself with such low-class people.

Sooner or later I had gotten switched out to only be working with the gifted education teacher, but I didn't learn Math, Science, English or the regular subjects kids learned, I learned about black holes. My learning had stopped, and after a while, I had become lonely. Lonely because I learned whoever was my friend, was only using me for my head. Lonely because I was isolated. Lonely because it was done to me by both my teachers and peers. After, I stopped caring and gained an ego helping me cope with why I didn't need them in my life.

Fast forward to 4th grade, I'm back in the regular education class and I did my best to try to get rid of the "ego." Now my idea of changing became that I needed those people in my life, and no matter how smart I was, I needed them. As a teen now, I have come to the realization that human beings value assimilation over exclusion. So as a fourth grader, I chose my teachers and peers oven an education. Thinking back, I still don't know if I made the right decision. People or education, it's a hard argument even now.

The reason why I wanted to tell you this story is because I want you to know how desperate I had become because I wanted friends over my education. I wanted to explain where any resentment towards people had started, especially towards my teachers and peers and to explain how much I really do appreciate you and your class. Here I met new friends who became teachers, and I have a teacher who is willing to be a friend, and you don't find that a lot in the world.

So how I wanted to end this letter is with this: I had some bad experiences in my life, and for a long time I didn't really like who I was. I held resentment towards myself, teachers and peers. I was lonely and lost but as I grew older I learned to respect the people around me, and I have you as one of the many things to thank for changing my way of thinking. So, thank you.

Sincerely,
Gifted & Lonely

SUPER APPRECIATIVE

Dear Teacher,

Throughout this year, I have achieved many of my goals I have set for this class and I can't wait to achieve more. As a student of yours, I'm very appreciative of the things you share with us from your personal life and the things you do for us in class. You show from the inside out that you truly care for us and for the decisions we're about to make in the near future. For many years I had never had an Asian teacher to show me my ways and how to understand life from another perspective. When I had White teachers, they always talked so highly about how they achieved their goals and how we will too, if we just believe. But what they didn't tell us was how hard it was going to be because of our racial makeup and how race could hold us back.

Looking back, I was held up in a tiny era, where I didn't have many options to make. Some of my teachers couldn't relate to me, like how I would come home to 3 younger siblings and take care of them as if they were my children. Making sure my siblings ate enough, so they didn't feel like they had to ration food. Showering them so they didn't have the stench of yesterday's smell. While my parents were busy making money to put food on the table and clothes on our bodies, I was the parent in the house making sure my younger siblings felt warm and taken care of in the house.

What motivates me is my dad. He motivates me because as a child growing up in Thailand, it was hard for him. He would always tell me that he didn't have specific supplies he needed, and he was raised in a big family so money was a problem. Whenever my dad tells me his stories back in Thailand, I get sad because he didn't have many opportunities. When I asked him why he wanted to come to America, I can see it on his face that America is a hero to him where he can achieve goals that he couldn't back to Thailand. However, when I ask him if he misses Thailand, he responds to me, "Of course. Even though I came to America, Thailand is my home."

Another person that motivates me is my cousin. She is 19 years old and currently attends college. Even though she is many miles away from me, I still look up to her. My cousin has always helped inspired me to thrive more each day. She graduated with high honors from high school and that is what inspired me. I was inspired to aspire because she has achieved so many goals and continues to thrive more each day. My cousin has shared about her struggles in college to me, and she has helped me set my mindset to the path that helps me grow and learn more.

The struggles that I have faced and currently still face is my mental self. I hear my voice wanting to break down and cry because sometimes when the days are not as bright as the others, I just want to shut down and give up. I have this realization even if I do achieve my goals, I wouldn't have enough money to do what I want to. My family has other kids to focus on, and my brother will soon be attending college after me. As the oldest, I feel obligated to give up what I have, so my younger siblings can be able to achieve their dreams and goals. I hope this voice of mine fades away as I begin to succeed.

The goals I want to achieve is graduating my junior year with high honors, so I can start PSEO. I want to take Drivers Ed class, so I can drive back and forth to school and college. After high school I want to go to college out of Minnesota so I can be exposed to many more options. I love filmmaking and photography, so I want to major in something that involves those. My dream job is to become a prosecutor, for I love solving mysteries and I find it very intriguing. But I want to be realistic here, so I hope to get a job that involves photography.

If I don't go to college outside of Minnesota, I will probably go to a community college and get an apartment and live with my younger sister. I hope to be able to drive my sister and her friends around to let her experience things that I never got to do. Having you as a supportive teacher has really helped me in a truly genuine way. You hold up supportive arms for us to fall back into when we're not feeling the easiest. You help shape us and show us the way and I can't thank you enough for opening up my eyes to a better future. As many times as I say this, it still will not be enough, but thank you teacher for everything you do.

Sincerely,
Super Appreciative

HUNGRY FOR CONFIDENCE

Dear Teacher,

I'm glad I could share some things about me with you, to share some things I never told a single teacher in my 15 years of education. I have a large family, including my dog, so life is tough. I have to make time for chores for my siblings and parents every day, be a mother to my siblings, work hard at school, so I could get A's and B's, and on top of that learn how to mature and do things on my own. I have a lot of responsibilities as the oldest daughter in my family. Since there is so much stuff I have to balance in my life, I get stressed and frustrated and sometimes I feel like giving up on everything.

I had so many things to do at home, I hardly went out as a kid. I didn't get a chance to do what all the other kids have done as a kid. I wish you knew that as I grew up, I had really high expectations to meet and heard comments from other people. It started when I was between the age of nine and ten. I was a kid who pretty much understood how to feel bad about myself, to let all these comments into my head, and I tried to put a lot of effort to change myself, just so I can be that perfect person everyone wants me to be.

I wish you knew that I grew up being afraid of what people had to say about me, think about me, and I even was scared that I wouldn't fit in with anyone. Along with that, I have social anxiety. I fear so many things, and I didn't know how to make any new friends, or I wasn't given opportunities to speak to my peers to develop social skills. In addition, when I go out, I start to panic whenever a stranger talks to me. I never got to experience the real world and how to talk to strangers properly.

I wish you knew that I'm not so confident in myself. I fear that I'm not a good Hmong daughter. I fear that if I don't have good grades, I will not be a good role model for my siblings. Yes, I know my life is like every typical Hmong girl's life. You may think that it's normal while I think it's different. All these bad comments and put-downs had really made me think negatively about myself. At this time, I was even depressed from all the things I had to handle on my own, everything I heard from people, and things which have been inside me for such a long time. So yes, I fear someone's judgment and opinions about me. Furthermore, all those things have really changed me and who I am. I thank you for listening to what I wanted to say.

Sincerely,
Hungry for Confidence

STEPPING STONE

Dear Teacher,

Here are some things I hope you know about me and consider when looking at me as your student.

First of all, I'm currently a part-time PSEO student and I'm learning how to balance high school and college workloads. I'm starting to get a hang of it, but I'm still in the learning process; therefore, if I ever seem stressed or daydreaming, I'm probably thinking about school. It's not that I'm bored in class or disrespecting you in anyway, but I'm trying to change and grow with the workload, responsibilities, etc. as they are pushed upon me.

The next thing I would like you to know is learning Hmong is still a learning progress for me. I feel like I may be still a beginner at some things like writing, and intermediate at certain things like listening. Therefore, I don't want to be labeled into a group when we do separate, because my Hmong skills vary.

One of the last things I want you to know about me is as of right now I'm trying to get into more women empowerment related things. I attended something that has really changed my mind about this topic. If you know any programs or clubs that deal with this kind of stuff, it would be greatly appreciated if you let me know. I want to be able to speak out for minority women in particular, because it's something that I have heard is a real struggle and I want to be able to break that cycle that we have to go through.

I would like to say I have grown a lot as a person in a short amount of time. I feel like I now know so much more about myself then I did before. I know what I want, stand by, and who I need by my side in order to achieve what I want. Because of this, I'm proud that I try to be more involved and meet new people because this was one of those stepping stones I needed to do before doing anything else. I'm breaking out of those stereotypes which have been labeled upon Hmong kids. I want to be that person to do it and I just need some courage and confidence to do so. However, I know I can and will do this because I feel an inner calling within me to do these kinds of things.

Lastly, I want to talk and share about updates from my previous letter I wrote as a freshman. I'm still living with my mom and visiting my dad every now and then. The idea and stress level which I used to have their divorce has decreased and I no longer stress about it. I guess in a way I have just gotten used to it as more things happened in the previous year. Another update I have is my reason why I chose to continue Hmong 2, even though I was planning to quit this year. I decided to continue this because I know being in this class has changed my perception of being Hmong and I know this class has really helped me learn and progress in my Hmong, which is something I'm really proud of because I'm not as lost as I was about the Hmong before. I still think about joining the pageant here and there, but I'm not sure. The last update I have for you is that I'm still that hard working and driven person I have always been. Except like what I said earlier, I know what I want now so I'm more careful of what I really need to strive and work for. For now, this concludes my letter to you my teacher, however there may be more to add later on.

Sincerely,
Stepping Stone

THINKING TOO MUCH

Dear Teacher,

There are many things I wished you know about me, but here are three.

First, I love my Boy Scout troop like my family. The reason behind this is that I grew up with the Boy Scout troop, just like my brothers did when they went to it. I have been in Boy Scouts for about 4 years now, and I'm currently ranked at a Life Scout position, which is the rank just below Eagle Scout. This means a lot to me because Eagle Scout is the final and highest rank you can get as a Boy Scout, so it will be the last thing I accomplish as a Boy Scout. To be honest, going for Eagle Scout is a scary and happy feeling to me. I ask myself, "What am I going to do after I achieve Eagle Scout? Am I just going to quit and do nothing for the troop anymore, or am I going to get off my butt and work hard for the troop to continue progressing." Also, Boy Scouts give me a sense of direction of what to do and what not to do, as well as what is good and what is bad. Boy Scouts has had one of the biggest impacts on me. When I go to Boy Scouts, I can express myself in any way I think is normal, and they won't laugh at me for it. What they will actually do, instead of laughing at you, is accept you for who you are. It makes me teary just typing this because, at school, I can't express myself how I want to express myself, like I do at Boy Scouts and at home. At school, trying to show your true self to people will only get them to laugh or ignore you forever, and it even makes me go away in disgust. I get sad that no one wants to know me as a person, as a friend.

Sometimes I don't know how to control what I do and how I feel. This topic is quite hard for me to discuss. When I get angry, sad or happy, I tend to do more of what has become expected of me. For instance, when I get angry, I step out of line and bring others' personal lives into the conversation. I also act like I know nothing of the situation, and it still hurts them inside. Sometimes, I get so angry to the point that I can't be angry anymore, and I will just go somewhere that I can't be bothered and cry out my anger. Now, this is where my emotions start to get out of control. After I cry, I begin to question my existence, like: "Why am I here? Why does it have to be me? Where do I go when I die?" Then, my questions grow darker and darker as I continue to question myself, "Will my friends forget me when I die? How come my friends are with their other friends? Was I the one who drove them away? Why I do feel so lonely when I'm with friends?" Then my questions gets as dark as it can be…. "Why should I be alive, when I make everything worse?" I'm sorry if I made this letter feel very depressing. I guess I do make everything worse anyways.

That brings me to my last thing I want you teachers to know about me. I like to think and space out a lot. Now, you might have gotten this from the last one, but when I'm bored or need to cool down, I actually just think about what something is and what the mysteries of the earth are. I usually just think about how I am going to do in college, something in the future that I might take an interest in or something in the past that I could have done better. My emotions usually go back into the past, where I think of what I could have done.

If I didn't focus on girls, then I focused on academics. That is the reason why I have these thoughts and why I'm hurt forever. There was a girl that has opened up my mind that girls are just a distraction from my sadness. Just so you know, I tend not to have a lover. Perhaps, forever. Just my experience, so I don't want to get hurt again. Then again, maybe I'm the one who has hurt others, and she didn't say anything about it. Maybe I'm the one who did all the horrible things? Maybe it was me who was the problem, and not her? Maybe, it's better this way? Maybe…. Maybe……Maybe, I'm just not good enough to be her partner, so I let her go, so she can go find someone even better than me….

Finally, I have done something good for that relationship. I hope she is doing great today, even though it pains me to see her go. Sorry, I just make everything worse than it was before, don't I? I guess, that is something that will never change about me.

Sincerely,
Thinking Too Much

Bring Out the Best in Me

Dear Teacher,

I wish you knew how hard expectations are for the oldest child in Hmong families. The things the oldest child has to go through, such as stress and high expectations are for you. Whenever I make a mistake or when I act not like a guy, I get lectured for hours and hours until my parents are done explaining their life story, like they had something to achieve. I always knew I try my best to fulfill the tasks they ask to the best of my capabilities. I wish you knew how much sadness I carry with me everyday living without a father and having your only other sibling live with the other parent. I wish you knew how much stress I had to take, and how much discipline I needed for seven years to have endured all this pain to keep improving myself as a young male adult.

I wish you knew that I'm a slow learner. It takes time for me to retain new information. I wish you knew that I'm afraid of getting up in big groups and having to present something, or do a speech of some sort and how it affects my vocal capabilities when speaking in English or another language. I have to see, listen to instructions on how to do something, or vocally say something. I wish you knew that failing takes a heavy toll on me and stresses me out, and I get anxiety to redo or re-take a task or assignment.

I wish you knew how lazy I am. I'm disciplined, but don't have any willpower to do anything. For example, if I'm forcing myself to do something, I will get it done, but when it comes to my own decision, I will take the easy way out and try not to do anything challenging. If an assignment is given in class I will try my best to get it done in class as soon as possible. This is something I wish you knew about me, so you can help bring out the best in me.

Sincerely,
Bring Out the Best in Me

❋+❋+❋+❋+❋+❋+❋+❋+❋+❋+❋+❋+❋+❋

Muaj Lub Laj Lim Tswv Yim Zoo

Nyob Xibfwb,
Kuv yog ib tug ntxhais Hmoob kawm ntawv nyob rau hauv Park Center Senior High. Xyoo no kuv kawm ntawv nyob rau qib kaum ob lawm. Tsis ntev no xwb ces twb yuav kawm tiav lawm tiag. Lub neej yav pem suab tseem tshuav ntev heev thiab tseem yuav muaj ntau yam uas yuav tshwm sim. Txawv yuav zoo li cas los yus yuav tsum tau xav txog lub neej yav tas los hais tias yus tau los deb npaum li cas lawm.

Kuv niam thiab kuv txiv yug nyob rau teb chaws Nplog. Thaum

lub caij ua tsov ua rog, nkawv thiaj li khiav los rau Thaib teb thiab los nyob rau hauv Vib Nais. Kuv yog tus ntxhais yau thib ob nyob rau hauv kuv tsev neeg. Kuv yug nyob rau hauv Thaib teb. Tom qab yug peb cov nus muag tag, kuv txiv tau txais ib tug mob tsis zoo ces ho tau tso peb tseg lawm. Nyob rau xyoo ob phav plaub, kuv niam lawv thiaj li txiav txim siab mus xam phaj thiab tuaj rau teb chaws Meskas.

Thaum tuaj txog Meskas lawm, peb tsev neeg tau txais txoj kev txom nyem heev vim hais tias ib pob nyiaj los tsis muaj, ib tug ntawv los tsis paub thiab ntsia qhov twg los luag tsis yog yus tej txheeb tej ze li. Kuv niam tau txiav txim siab mus noj nyiaj laus thiab mus txais nyiaj muas noj hos kuv tus niam laus hlob thiab tus nus hlob tau mus kawm ntawv thiab ua hauj lwm txhawm los pab them nuj nqis thiab yuav zaub mov noj. Peb cov tom qab tseem yau yau ces peb tsuas yog hais tias niaj hnub mus kawm ntawv xwb.

Hais txog ntawm kuv lub neej thaum tseem me me, kuv tau mus kawm ntawv nyob rau ob peb lub tsev kawm ntawv Hmoob. Kuv tau kawm nyob rau peb lub tsev kawm ntawv Hmoob. Vim hais tias tag nrho cov tsev kawm ntawv nov yog Hmoob, kuv thiaj tau kawm tau ntawv Hmoob zoo. Nyob rau qib ob, kuv tau mus sib tw xeem Spelling Bee nyob rau pem Concordia hos nyob rau qib xya thiab yim, kuv tau mus nrog kuv cov phooj ywg seev cev nyob rau tim tshiab peb caug.
Tom qab uas kuv kawm tiav lawm, kuv thiaj tau mus kawm nyob rau lub tsev kawm ntawv no thaum qib cuaj. Thaum kuv mus kawm nyob rau lub tsev kawm ntawv tshiab lawm, txhua yam txawv tag nrho. Yus tau mus pib dua txoj kev taug tshiab, yuav tau mus ua phoojywg tshiab thiab tau mus ntsib cov xibfwb tshiab.

Txoj kev kawm ntawv yeej tsis yog hais tias yuav nyuaj pes tsawg tabsis kuv tau txais txoj kev nyuaj siab los ntawm kuv tsevneeg thiab kuv lub neej nyob rau pem tsev. Nyob rau hauv kuv tsev neeg tam sim no, kuv nyob nrog kuv ob tug nus hlob thiab peb tug vivncaus nrog rau kuv niam.

Ho lwm cov ces twb tau mus muaj lub neej tag lawm. Thaum uas kuv txiv tau xiam tag, es peb tau tuaj rau tebchaws Meskas lawm, kuv niam thiaj rov yuav dua ib tug txiv tshiab. Ob peb xyoos tom qab ntawv, nkawv tau ua lub neej tsis sib haum ces nkawv thiaj li sib nrauj lawm thiab. Tom qab uas sib nrauj tag, kuv niam thiaj rov mus yuav dua ib tug. Qhov uas nws rov yuav dua ib tug es txiav txim siab tso lub npe poj nrauj tseg los vim yog nws xav kom peb cov me nyuam rov qab mus txais peb lub xeem qub. Thiab ib qho ntxiv, kuv niam yog ib tug tib neeg uas tsis nyiam nrog lwm tus muaj teeb meem. Nws nyiam nyob raws txoj kev ywj pheej thiab kajsiab nkaus xwb. Vim feem ntau cov tib neeg Hmoob yog ib hom uas nyiam muaj lus xaiv thiab lus hais. Yog koj tsis muaj ib tug txij tug nkawm ces lawv ntshai ntshai tsam koj ho nyiam mus tham lawv tus txij tus nkawm.

Ob peb xyoos tom qab uas kuv niam thiab txiv tshiab nkawv sib yuav lawm peb thiaj li rov tau sawv hauv lub qhov taub los. Mus rau tej txheeb tej ze los lawv thiaj saib tau peb dua thiab hwm peb dua. Tabsis ntshe yeej yog txoj hmoo thiab los xyov yog ua li cas, kuv txiv tshiab tsis ua lub siab ncaj ncees rau kuv niam. Nws tau rov mus tham dua ib tug uas ho yog peb ib tug txheeb tug ze kiag thiab xwb.

Thaum uas kuv txiv tshiab tau mus lawm es tsis tshua los tsev, kuv niam ho tau txais ib tug mob tsis zoo. Twb kho npaum li cas los pheej tsis txawj zoo li ces lawv thiaj li mus tsawv neeb seb puas yog tim tej dab qhuas. Thaum uas ntaus nraus es pom tau hais tias kuv niam tshee tshee, lawv thiaj li paub hais tias yog kuv niam yuav ua neeb. Tom qab ntawv, kuv niam thiaj li pib zoo zuj zus.

Thaum uas kuv niam paub txog kuv txiv, nkawv thiaj li muaj teeb meem me ntsis ces thiaj li tau sib nrauj. Tom qab uas sib nrauj tag, kuv txiv tshiab ntawv thiaj li tau mus yuav tus poj niam ntawv los ua tus niam yau thiab ho tau rov tuaj thov kuv niam yuav dua thiab. Xyoo ntawv yog ib xyoo uas nyuaj siab thiab ntxhov plawv tshaj plaws nyob rau hauv peb lub neej. Vim hais tias kuv niam cov me nyuam tsuas xav kom peb nyob luag ntxhi thiab kaj siab lug. Tabsis nws ho tseem xav tuav nws lub npe dua. Thaum kawg nkawv thiaj li rov sib yuav dua lawm.

Peb tsev neeg yog ib pab uas tau mus nrog cov Hmoob ua teb thiab tau mus muag zaub thiab. Nyob rau lub caij ntuj no ces ho mus kawm ntawv hos thaum txog lub caij ntuj sov ces yuav mus ua teb thiab muag khoom nyob rau tom kiab tom khw. Nov yog ib txoj kev uas khwv tshaj plaws vim hais tias yus twb ntshaw ntshaw kom tau koom ib lub caij ntuj sov tiag tiag ib yam li lwm tus thiab los ua li cas yus tsuas tau mus tiv tshav tiv nag nkaus nkaus xwb. Tej thaum yus twb xav yaum yus cov vivncaus mus ua si saib vaj tsiaj los yog mus ncig tebchaws thiab lwm qhov los thaum kawg yus yeej paub hais tias tsis muaj ib lub caij nyoog uas yuav tau so li ntawv li.

Hais txog ntawm kuv tus kheej, yam uas kuv nyiam ua thaum kuv tsis muaj dabtsi ua lawm yog kos duab, muab khoom sib txiav, coj los sib dhos thiab sib nplaum ua ke. Tsis tas li ntawv xwb kuv kuj nyiam xaws khaub ncaws thiab ua paj ntaub raws rau txoj kev lom zem. Kuv kuj nyiam nyiam mus yuav paj dag thiab nplooj ntoo dag coj los txiav thiab dai rau hauv kuv lub hoob txaj kom zoo nkauj thiab tshiab khiv. Yog kuv tso paj rau hauv kuv lub hoob ces nws ua rau kuv kaj siab dua.

Kuv niam tau hais rau kuv hais tias kuv yog ib tug tibneeg uas muaj lub laj lim tswv yim zoo thiab txawj ntse rau lub sij hawm thaum lwm tus lub tswv yim tws tas. Thaum uas kuv pib xaws khaub ncaws tuaj, kuv tsuas yog ntsia lwm tus xaws, kawm cov qauv khaub ncaws thiab tsuas kawm los ntawm kuv tus kheej thaum kuv ua yuam kev xwb. Muaj ob peb zaug uas kuv niam tsis nco qab hais tias yog nws muab tej khoom tso qhov twg los yog hais tias pawv lawm ces, kuv yeej yog tus mus nrhiav tau tas li xwb. Tej thaum kuv muab xav txog ces nws yeej txaus ntshai tsawv thiab txawv kawg nkaus.

Ib qhov txog ntawm kuv tus kheej uas kuv tsis nyiam tshaj plaws

92

yog vim hais tias kuv yog ib tug neeg uas nquag nquag muaj mob. Kuj tsis yog hais tias muaj mob loj tabsis kuv yog ib tug tib neeg uas muaj qhov dias taub hau, hnoos thiab mob plab noj mov tsis haum tas li xwb. Thaum uas kuv nco tau tias kuv yog ib tug neeg uas hnoos hnoos yog thaum kuv nyob hoob peb los lawm. Tej thaum, kuv yeej tu tu siab hais tias ua li cas yus ho tsis zoo li lwm tus es yuav tsis muaj mob li tabsis yog kuv ho xav haistias twb muaj ib co neeg tseem muaj ntau yam kev nyuaj tshaj yus ces ua rau kuv kaj siab zog.

Ib yam uas kuv ntshai tshaj plaws nyob hauv lub qab ntuj no yog kuv ntshai tsam kuv yuav tau plam cov neeg uas kuv hlub thiab tshua. Tus ib yog kuv niam. Ib leej niam txoj kev hlub uas muab rau nws cov me nyuam yog ib txoj kev hlub uas loj tshaj plaws thiab tsis muaj ib yam dabtsi yuav los piv tau los yog txhais tau. Kuv yeej nkag siab hais tias muaj ib hnub kuv niam yeej yuav tau tso lub ntiaj teb no tseg. Es nws yuav tsis nrog kuv nyob mus ib txhis. Tabsis yog muab xav los ces tu tu lub siab. Yog tsis muaj yus niam lawm es leej twg thiaj li yuav los ua yus niam? Thaum rov qab los txog tsev es leej twg yuav hu yus lub npe tias me naib?

Kuv lub hom phiaj uas tseem ceeb tshaj plaws rau kuv yog kuv yuav tsum tau ntxiv rov qab txoj kev hlub uas kuv niam tau muab rau kuv thiab nws cov me nyuam. Kuv xav tau ib txoj haujlwm kom tau nyiaj ntau, yuav ib lub tsev, thiab caw kuv niam mus nrog kuv nyob yam ywj siab hlo. Qhov nov yog kuv lub hom phiaj. Yog li ntawv, kuv thiaj yuav tsum tau mus kawm ntawv thiab ua hauj lwm.

Tom qab uas kuv kawm tiav xyoo no qib kaum ob, kuv cia siab hais tias kuv yuav tsum tau mus caum cuag kuv txoj kev npau suav thiab lub hom phiaj. Kuv txoj kev npau suav thiab lub hom phiaj ntawv yog mus kawm nyob rau qib siab kom tau ib daim degree. Tsawg kawm los yuav tsum tau daim Bachelor's. Thaum nkawm ntawv los yuav tsum tau ua hauj lwm thiab, kom tau nyiaj los pab txhawm rau txoj kev kawm, nuj nqis, thiab kom tau lub laj lwm tswv rau lwm txoj hauj lwm lub neej yav pem suab. Kuv txoj kev npau suav uas kuv ntshaw tshaj plaws yog mus kawm ua ib tug tib neeg tsim khoom coj los muag los yog hu ua eutreperneur. Kuv xav ua ib tug tswv ntawm ib lub tablaj loj loj. Tab sis qhov no tsuas yog kuv txoj kev npau suav xwb, xyov nws puas yuav los txog thiab. Yog hais tias kuv mus tsis tau li kuv txoj kev xav ces, kuv xav mus ua ib tug neeg muab tshuaj los yog kws kho mob pab tib neeg.

Sau Npe,
Muaj Lub Laj Lim Tswv Yim Zoo

꠸꠸꠸꠸꠸꠸꠸꠸꠸꠸꠸꠸꠸꠸꠸

Yuav Dai Hauv Kuv Lub Siab

Nyob Zoo Xibfwb,
Koj yeej paub ntau ntau yam txog kuv lawm tias sis tseem muaj ntau ntau yam ua koj tsis tau paub. Cov koj tsis tau paub ces yog ntawm kuv tus kheej thiab kuv txoj kev xav. Kuv tsis muaj phooj ywg ntau vim hais tias kuv ntshai tsam lawv txiav txim siab ua neeg phem es tsis nyiam kuv los hais lus phem rau kuv. Kuv nyiam nyob ib leeg xwb vim hais tias nyob ib leeg ces tsis muaj kev nyuaj siab losis tsis muaj kev kuam siab. Thaum kuv tseem me, kuv muaj muaj mob thiab mus haus maus ntau xwb vim qhov ntawd kuv tsis tshuam nyiam rog neeg vim thaum me.

Hauv kuv tsev neeg, kuv yawg thiab kuv pog mus yug kuv txiv hauv teb chaws Nplog. Kuv yawg mus ua tub rog thaum nws muaj caum tsib xyoo xwb. Thaum lawv mus rau hauv Thaib teb, lawv mus xya hnub mam li mus txog. Txhuas txhuas hnub yeej los los nag heev. Ib ob xyoo thom qab, lawv tuaj txog teb chaws Mekas. Thaum kuv txiv pib tiav hluas

94

nraug lawm, kuv yawg yuam kom nws mus kawm ntawv siab kom mus kawm tau nws diam master's degree. Tag nrog kuv cov phauj, cov yawg laus, thiab kuv pog, ntxub ntxub kuv yawg heev tiam sis kuv yawg tsis xav li cas vim hais tias nws paub nws qhov kev xav rau kuv txiv yog qhov uas zoo tshaj rau nws tus tub lub neej.

Ntawm kuv ces yeej muaj kev nyuaj siab ntau vim hais tias kuv txiv zoo ib yam kuv yawg. Kuv txiv xav kom kuv mus kawm ntawv siab kom muaj nyiaj ntau ntau. Kuv ces kuv xav mus kawm ntawv siab tiam sis kuv xav mus kawm qhov kuv nyiam. Nyiaj ntawm kuv ces tsis tseem ceeb vim hais tias nyiaj yuav tsis ua koj zoo siab los kaj siab. Kuv paub hais tias kuv niam thiab kuv txiv hlub hlub kuv heev li thiab lawv txoj kev xav rau kuv lub neej yog qhov zoo xwb, kuv thiaj li txiav txim siab ua qhov lawv nyiam thiab qhov lawv xaiv cia rau kuv pib thaum kuv tseem yau. Kuv yuav tsis hais qhia rau lawv vim hais tias qhia ces kuv ntshai tsam lawv tus siab rau kuv. Kuv xav kom lawv zoo siab xwb.

Kuv tsev neeg thiab kuv tsis tsuas tham lus thiab nrog tib leeg ua ke vim hais tias thaum kuv me, kuv niam thiab kuv txiv mus ua hauj lwm ntau ntau thiab cia kuv tus nus yau thiab kuv mus rau kuv pog zov xwb. Thaum kuv tseem me, kuv tsis paub ntau txog kuv tsev neeg losis kuv niam thiab kuv txiv vim hais tias tsis muaj leej twg qhia kuv tiam sis tam sis no kuv loj hlob lawm ces tag nrog cov teeb meem hauv kuv tsev neeg, kuv yawg qhia tag nrog rau kuv xwb. Kuv niam thiab kuv txiv, yeej tsis hais dab tsi mus txog hnub no.

Kuv txoj kev tu siab ces yog ntawm kuv tsev neeg vim hais tias muaj ntau ntau yam ua tsis zoo hauv kuv tsev neeg. Kuv tu siab vim hais tias kuv txiv xav hais tias kuv yawg tsis hlub nws tiam sis qhov ntawm tsis muaj tseeb. Kuv yawg yeej hlub kuv txiv tag nws txoj siab. Kuv txiv yog kuv yawg txoj kev zoo siab tiam sis kuv qhia tsis tau rau kuv txiv vim hais tias thaum nws txiav txim siab xav ib qho ces kuv yuav ua tsis tau dab tsi ua yuav hloog nws txoj kev xav.

Kuv txoj kev zoo siab ces yeej ho yog kuv tsev neeg vim hais tias lawv hlub kuv thiab yug kuv loj hlob. Lawv pab txhawb nqa kuv thiab qhia kuv txoj cov koom uas zoo losis rau cov koom ua tsis zoo. Kuv zoo siab hais tias txawm kuv tsev neeg tsis zoo meej los tsuav peb txawj sib hlub thiab sib pab. Yeej muaj txuas hnub ua tsis zoo tiam sis tseem muaj ntau ntau hnub ua yeej zoo thiab. Kuv xav hais tias kuv yeej muaj muaj mob vim hais tias kuv tau ib tse neeg ua zoo tshaj plaws li. Txawm kuv tsis muaj ntau yam lus zoo los kuv lub neej yeej zoo tiam sis tag nrog cov phem hauv kuv lub neej yeej yuav dai hauv kuv lub siab.

Tag nrog kuv lub neej kuv yuav tsis muab qhia rau leej twg vim hais tias kuv qhia ces kuv yuav quaj xwb. Kuv lam hais qhia thiab sau me me rau hauv diam ntawv no rau koj nyeem xwb. Yeej tseem muaj ntau ntau yam uas kuv tsis tau qhia. Thov kom koj tsis txhob xav dab tsi. Xav paub ntxiv ces noog kuv tau. Tsis xav paub los kuv tsis xav li cas.

Tsis xav dab tsi losis thaum peb tham lus hauv hoob Hmoob no, kuv yeej yuav mam qhia me me txog kuv lub neej kom phim qhov lus noog. Kuv xau li no xwb vim hais tias sau ntau ces laj laj nyeem thiab tus siab xwb.

Sau Npe,
Yuav Dai Hauv Kuv Lub Siab

Txhua Yam Tsis Nyuaj Lawm

Nyob zoo Xibfwb,

Ua ntej no kuv yuav qhia koj txog kuv lub neej. Kuv yuag los rau ib tsev neeg ua hais lus Hmoob thiab lus Mekas, tiam si thaum kuv tseem me kuv hais lus Hmoob ntau xwb. Thaum hais txog hais lus Hmoob ntawm cov me nyuam hau, kuv tsev neeg, kuv yog tus hais lus Hmoob ntau tshaj. Kuv paub nyeem ntawv Hmoob thiab kuv yeej txawj sawv ntawv Hmoob. Kuv yuav qhia koj ob pes los txog kuv txoj kev kawm ntawv. Txij thaum kuv pib kawm ntawv kuv mloog zoo li kuv kawm npaum cas los kuv yeej kawm tsis laib li. Hnub no kuv nyob rau hau qib kaum ib, txhua yam rau kuv tsis nyuaj rau kuv lawm.

Kuv yog ib tug ntxhais ua nyiam hu suab nkauj heev. Kuv twb sau tau 1-2 txoj nkauj tiam sis tsis tau muab los kaw tseg xwb. Ib xyoo mas ntev kawg. Thaum lub kaum ib hlis ntuj kuv yeej mus hu nkauj rau tom Hmoob Xyooj lub tshiab peb caug. Thaum lub caij ntuj sov, kuv nyiam kawm xaws xyaum paj ntaub tiam sis kuv twb tsis txawj ua paj ntaub li. Cov no yog ib co khoom uas kuv ua tau lub caij ntuj sov.

Kuv lub neej yav pem suab kuv xav mus kawm lub tsev kawm ntawv rau ib lub University fab nursing rau hau cov me nyuam thiab niam los si ib tug obstetrician. Tsis tag li ntawm xwb kuv xav mus kawm kom tau kuv daim Master's degree thiab Doctorate. Kom thaum kuv muaj me nyuam thiab thaum kuv yuav txiv kuv thiaj li tsis txom nyem. Tam si no kuv twb pib xav txog kuv lub neej lawm hais tias kuv yuav ua dab tsi kom kuv lub neej zoo thiaj li tsis txom nyem heev. Kuv daim ntawv los sau li no xwb, tsis tshua muaj dab tsis hais txog lawm vim hais tias txhua yam ua kuv ua tam si no tseem zoo li qub.

Mus Nyob Zoo Koj,
Txhua Yam Tsis Nyuaj Lawm

HLUAS NRAUG KAUSLIM ZOO NRAUG

Nyob zoo Xibfwb,

Xib fwb, kuv xav qhia rau koj hais txog kuv qhov npau suav. Koj twb paub tias kuv xav ua ib tug tib neeg uas hu nkauj thiab seev cev rau tim teb chaws Kauslim. Kuv xav ua heev vim rau qhov kuv nyiam mus pem lub sam thiaj vim rau qhov thaum tib neeg saib kuv seev cev, kuv zoo siab heev thiab kuv lom zem. Kuv twb kawm lus Kauslim thiab kuv paub sau ntawv thiab nyeem ntawv Kauslim thiab. Tab sis kuv xav tau kev pab vim rau qhov kuv tsis muaj ib lub dance studio losis mic zoo siv, thiab kuv xav tau ib daim iav loj loj vim rau qhov kuv pom kuv tus kheej seev cev. Nyuaj heeg os Xibfwb, tab sis kuv mas ua raws li kuv txog kev npau suav vim rau qhov no yog kuv tus npau suav.

Kuv paub tias thaum kuv cov pob kab ntxau ploj lawm, kuv yuav zoo li ib tug tub Kauslim zoo nraug heev. Thaum kuv saib Kdrama, kuv pom lawv kab lis kev cai thiab kuv kawm txog lawv cov lus. Yog tias kuv tos ntev dhau lawm, tus agency tim Kauslim tsis txais kuv vim rau qhov lawv hais tias thaum tib neeg me me li 15 xyoo ces yooj yim dua cov neeg laus.

Tiag tiag, kuv xav tau ib tug tib neeg pab kuv ua kuv tus manager losis tus pab kuv vim rau qhov kuv tsis paub ntau heev. Kuv xav tias lub company kuv xav mus audition yuav tsum yuav kuv vim rau qhov kuv twb kawm ntawv Kauslim ntau heev thiab kuv xyaum seev cev txhua txhua hnub. Kuv yuav tsum tau xyaum seev cev kom ntau tshaj no mus thaum kuv los txog hauv tsev vim rau qhov yog tias kuv muaj kev rau siab seev cev ces nws yuav pab kuv thaum kuv ua kuv diam audition video.

Xibfwb, kuv xav hais tias kuv yuav tsum tau kuv qhov audition xwb vim rau qhov kuv muab ntau lub sijhawm rau kev kawm lus Kauslim thiab kuv tws qhia txhua tus neeg hais tias kuv yuav ua ib tug K-pop idol thiab kuv yuav mus tim tej chaws Kauslim lawm. Tus tib neeg kuv qias no lawv qias kuv hais tias kuv yeej ua tau xwb.

Xib fwb, kuv xav hais tias ua tsaug vim rau qhov koj saib xyuas txog peb lub neeg. Qhov ntawv no pab kuv heev vim rau qhov kuv tsis muaj leeg tws hais li no rau kuv.

Sau Npe,
Hluas Nraug Kauslim Zoo Nraug

Tsis Xav Tau Dab Tsi Mus Ntxiv Lawm

Nyob Zoo Xibfwb,

Nyob hauv kuv lub neej kuv ib txwm muaj txoj kev xav hais tias kuv lub neej yuav tsis muaj txoj kev nyuaj siab tiam sis kuv muab xav mus xav los lub neej no nyuaj heev. Kuv yog ib tug ntxhais kawm uas nyiam nrog txhua leej txhua tus tham pem thiab yog ib tug neeg ua nyiam tso dag nrog txhua leej txhua tus tiam sis hauv kuv lub siab muaj kev nyuaj siab tsis paus tas. Lub neej no kuv lam muaj lub ntsej muag luag ntxhi xwb, tiam sis tiag tiag kuv tsuas muaj lub ntsej muag ua kua muag thwb los ntawm kuv ob sab plhu. Kuv muaj ob peb yam uas nyob hauv kuv lub siab kuv xav qhia rau koj puab.

Hnub kuv tau pib kawm ntawv nyob rau hauv high school, kuv lub siab xav kom kuv tau txoj kev hwm; ua cas kuv mus koom txhua lub club losis lawm cov event tsis zoo li kuv txoj kev npau suav. High school ua rau xav txog kuv lub neej tom ntej. Hauv kuv lub neej kuv yeej tsis muaj txoj kev lom zem, tsuas muaj kua muag thwb los xwb. Kuv muaj niam thiab txiv los zoo li tsis muaj. Mus kawm ntawv los kuv yeej muaj tes phooj ywg uas ncaws npas hais li hais. Yam kuv xav ua kuv yeej tsis tau ua vim hais tias kuv niam thiab txiv tsis cia kuv mus ncaws npas li kuv cov me phooj ywg. Kuv yeej tu siab heev vim kuv niam thiab txiv tsis zoo li lwm tus niam thiab txiv.

Vim kuv yug los ua ib tug me ntxhais hauv lub neej no, kuv thiaj li tsis tau mus ncaws npas los sis ua dab tsi lom zem li lwm tus tib neeg. Kuv yeej yog ib tug neeg ua xav los zem thiab ncaws npas tiam sis kuv yog ib tug ntxhais txoj hmoo tsis muaj kuv thiaj li tsis tau yam ntxawd. Yog ib tug ntxhais, kuv txoj hauj lwm yog tu tsev xwb, ua zaub ua mov noj tos kuv niam thiab kuv txiv lawv thiab mus kawm ntawv xwb. Ua cas yug los es yuav tau lub neej zoo li thaum kuv niam tseem nyob tim Laos. Kuv xav paub hais tias txhua tus niam puas zoo li ntxawd? Txoj kev mus ua nyab yeej tsis yooj yim thiab. Kuv yeej paus hais tias kuv yog ib tug ntxhais ua vwm rau txoj kev hlub tiam sis kuv tsis tau muaj txoj kev xav hais tias kuv yuav xav mus ua nyab. Txawm kuv tsis tau paub ua dab tsi ntau los kuv yeej paub me ntsis thiab nas. Kuv niam yeej hais rau kuv txhua hnub tias txoj kev uas kuv xav mus ncaws npas yuav tsis zoo rau kuv yog kuv mus ua lawv ib tug me nyab.

Muab xav mus xav los kuv yeej muaj txoj kev xav tias kuv niam thiab kuv txiv lawv puas muaj txoj kev cia siab rau kuv thiab? Paus yuas kam pab txhawb nqa kuv mus kom txog hnub uas kuv kawm ntawv tiav? Saib zoo li txij li thaum kuv nyob qib rau los kuv niam lawv yeej tsis pab txhawb nqa kuv lawm. Kuv tsis paub hais tias niam thiab txiv yeej zoo li ntawd losis tsuas muaj ib co niam txiv xwb.

Txoj kev sib hlub yeej tsis yooj yim li txhua leej txhua tus xav. Kev hlub tsis yog ib yam ua yuav ua si nrog. Txoj kev hlub yuav tsum mus kom kawg. Yog yuav hlub nrog ib tug neeg twb ces yeej yuav muaj txoj kev sib cav thiab tsis sib haum tiam sis thaum kawg ib tug yeej tsum zam txim rau ib tug xwb. Kuv yuav tsis dag kuv yeej yog ib tug neeg ua vwm rau txoj kev hlub tiam sis kuv yeej puab hais tias yog nws tsis hlub kuv, ces rov ua ib siab lawm xwb. Ntxawm lub siab yuav mob npaum li cas los kuv mam ua ib siab tso tus kuv hlub ntawd mus. Kuv yeej mob siab vim tsis muaj txoj kev hlub li lwm tus. Lam ua lub ntsej muag laug ntxhi xwb los yeej ua tsis tau txhua hnub vim tsuas muaj kua muag nrog txhua lub sijhawm.

Kuv lub neej yeej tsis zoo li txhua tus xav. Txawm kuv nyob nrog kua muag los lub siab yeej muaj txoj kev xav uas xav tau ib lub neej zoo thiab. Hauv kuv lub neej yeej tsis zoo npaum twb tiam sis thov kom cov me nyuam Hmoob tom ntej tsis txhob tau ib lub neej li kuv vim nws tu siab heev li. Rau kuv tus xib fwb uas tsis tau paub txog kuv txhua yam kuv yeej muab hais rau tsab ntawv no lawm. Kuv xav thov kom cov niam thiab txiv tiam sis no tsis txhob coj li thaum ub. Hauv teb chaws no, peb txawv tshaj yav dhau los lawm. Thaum koj nyeem tsab ntawv no, koj yeej paub lawm hais tias kuv nyuaj siab heev. Tsis muaj ib yam dab tsis ua rau kuv xav tau mus ntxiv lawm. Kuv yuav tsis hais ntau ntxiv lawm.

Sau Npe,
Tsis Xav Tau Dab Tsi Mus Ntxiv Lawm

Health

Food Dreams

Dear Teacher,

I wished my teacher knew that this lonely, humble girl at the front of class is hungry. I have been starving since the moment I woke up. I would love to eat lunch, but the lunch at school just is not my thing, and I find it nasty and disgusting. I pack unhealthy snacks, like cheesy puffs and soda, and that is what I eat in class. Still, I think about all the Korean food I want to eat, like black bean noodles, kimbap, bibimbap and spicy rice. Oh, so much food to think about! Writing this makes makes me feel so hungry.

I wish you knew that maybe kids are hungry, and they want to eat, but I know letting us bring food into class might attract mice. I would really love it, if you would allow such a great thing. I feel like it should be allowed because some people focus better with food, and we wouldn't be starving to death during the long 6 hours days we're here.

I would also want you to know that this impacts my learning too. If I'm hungry, then I wouldn't be able to focus in class and get those A's my strict parents ask for. I know that I'm overweight, and I should stop bringing snacks and sweet drinks into class, but I can't help it because I'm hungry. I will try to eat healthier and maybe bring 6 bell peppers, one for each class. Just to let you know that while you are teaching, I'm daydreaming about food.

Sincerely,
Food Dreams

ALWAYS GETTING HURT

Dear Teacher,

Right now, my family and I are in the middle of moving and the electricity in the bedrooms are dead. I can't charge my Chromebook in my room, so I have to charge it in the living room, and you know when you have younger siblings, they touch your things. So, I have to watch my Chromebook.

Last December, my grandma past away from tumor cancer in the morning at 6:00. The next day we didn't go to school because I was devastated. My grandma took care of me mostly when I was young. The thing I blamed myself for is when I didn't even go visit her when she was in the hospital until the last day. When I got there, she was sleeping. Her heart was still beating, but she wasn't getting up. Then the doctor said they will either try to help her even though she will not make it, or to make her comfortable for the last time. We couldn't make a choice until we told him to make her comfortable. Then I saw her pass. She never saw me come say "Hi."

There was this one time when I was riding bike down the street and I was going fast, and I wanted to turn around fast. That was the dumbest I have ever thought of because the bike slipped on gravel and I fell giving myself three scars, on my knee, two on my elbow. I got up, walked up the street to my grandma's house and told them I had fell. At the time my mom and grandma were going to the store, but when they saw me they canceled their trip. My grandma went and got a big jar of alcohol. The cut on my knee was too deep and the alcohol would make it hurt like hell. She put the alcohol on my elbow and it stung really bad, and after one day later I got a fever. I think it was from the knee because it got infected for one day as well. When my knee was kind of closing, she put alcohol on it and that one hurt the most out of all injuries of my life; I was crying because it hurt so much, and I couldn't do anything. Anyway, I'm telling you this because I get hurt and injured a lot. It happens once a week I don't know why, maybe it's bad luck? So, if you see me limping or cover a part of my body, then it means I'm hurt, but mostly it's not that bad, maybe it might just be a scrape.

Sincerely,
Always Getting Hurt

LIFE COMMUNICATOR

Dear Teacher,
Something I wished you knew about me is that I'm not always a quiet kid. The reason I'm so quiet is that I'm not really good at communicating with other people.

The second thing I wish you knew is that I'm having a hard time with school because I'm not used to being around people of different races, and I'm also not getting enough sleep from struggling with my homework.

The third thing I wished you knew about me is my life. I have been keeping secrets from friends and family for a long time. The reason I never told anyone is that I don't want any attention put on me. I don't like it when people ask about my life because I don't want my awful memories to come back. One of my secrets I will tell you is that when I was born, I almost died because I was too small and underweight. My mom and dad were really sad when they heard the news. The doctors did everything to keep me alive, so that I could have a future. These are all the things I wished my teachers knew. I'm glad that I'm still alive today because I found love, and I wish we have a future together.

Sincerely,
Life Communicator

STRUGGLING WITH LIVING LIFE

Dear Teacher,

I'm a quiet Hmong student who tries to get good grades in your class, but can't really speak, read, write or translate Hmong well. I'm pessimistic, but outgoing and introverted. I think I show the world how I want people to see me, but not how I personally see myself. I have struggled with living my life: How have I lived, who I am living it for, and for what purpose? I want you to know three things that I haven't yet shared with you or that you didn't know about me.

The first thing I want you to know is that I have suffered from some personal and mental health issues. I would wonder, "What's the purpose of being here if we all die in the end?" Honestly, I still don't know the answer to it. I still have panic attacks and anxiety when I have to present in class or if I'm blindfolded. When I'm blindfolded I would feel like I'm walking off a cliff and not know where I would go or if the next step is real or just my imagination.

The next thing I want you to know is how I have felt being compared to everyone my whole life and that I needed to reach high expectations to please everyone, including my family. My mom would always tell me to do good in school, which is expected from me, but when I try my best and I don't get "good grades" like "A's" then I wasn't good enough. In addition to that, I needed to work harder in school and for a while I would try and push myself so hard to reach my parents' expectations, to the point I would be sleep deprived and tired everyday and repeat the cycle each day. I felt like I have also been compared to people in height because I'm short. People would make fun of me or would tease me for being short or "not tall enough," especially for my age because I'm 4'11" at the age of 14. As well as being compared physically and academically, I also pushed myself mentally to try and be like my family because they are optimistic, outgoing, and friendly.

Lastly, I want you to know that I honestly don't know what I want to do in the future. I don't know what job I want, what college I want to go to, how long I want to go to college, what I want to study, and what I want to be when I grow up. Since I was young my mom would tell me to be something like a lawyer, doctor, or engineer. As I was growing up, I realized I followed what my parents wanted me to do, which doesn't fully allow me to know what I want to be. When I was young I wanted to be a dentist, but my mom would say, "You know you have to take care of people who have bad breath and ugly teeth?" And I would say "Yeah, I know." and nodded my head. As I grew up my mom would start saying how I should be an engineer, but I still wanted to be a dentist. Up until recently, I began to say, "I want to be an engineer or dentist," including that whenever someone asks what I want to be. I honestly don't know what I want to be.

Afterall, those are the few things that you didn't know about me.

Now that you have read my story, hopefully this will help you better understand me and when I struggle in class or in school.

Sincerely,
Struggling with Living Life

RISE UP

Dear Teacher,

I'm sure you already know I have a medical condition because I told you guys about it last year when the doctors didn't know how to fix it. I want to recap what happened to me in the past, and the signs that shows when I'm going into my episodes or mini seizures. When I was born I had a tumor inside me. I was fine since the tumor only made me hit puberty as a baby and the doctors had it all under control. Once I was twelve years old, the doctors gave me an all clear sign. I was fine after that until I turned sixteen. That was when I had my first seizure and then later on I started having mini-seizure left and right. The doctors didn't know what was wrong with me because when they did a brain scan on me, but my tumor didn't show any signs of being active at all, so they decided to have me take the first set of pills.

The pills had a powerful effect on me. Since I'm still young, they gave me the weakest dose of it, so I wouldn't fall asleep or get dizzy. Sadly, the first set of pills didn't work since I was still getting my mini-seizures a lot, so the doctors decided to give me a stronger dose. It didn't work either, but the good thing was that I wasn't having a lot of mini-seizures. It was still happening once in awhile, so the doctors brought me to a testing area to see if it's my brain waves that were the reasons why I was having mini-seizures, but my brain waves were fine. The doctors decided to give me a stronger pill again, and so once I took the new pills it worked because the only time I had my mini-seizure was when I was helping my brother with something. After that I don't recall ever having one again.

My brother still thinks we still have to watch out for me because we both think the main reason why I'm having them is stress. So, the signs to know if I'm having a mini-seizure is if I start acting really weird, like start acting like a crab, or when talking to me, if I respond in a weird way. Or start talking about something random and super out of topic then that is when I'm having one. If I ask you, "What happened?" or "Did I black out?" then that is a sign that I had it while in class.

Life is challenging and stressful because I have to watch out for myself and I hate making my family worry and stress out about me. My mom can't sleep at night that well anymore because she is worried about me having a seizure and that no one will be able to help me when I have one. I keep telling her that I will be alright, but even I worry about myself sometimes. Even if this challenge is hard, I wouldn't let it get to me that easily. I shall rise up and face it until the challenge is over!

Sincerely,
Rise Up

ALMOST LOST MY VISION

Dear Teacher,

When I was very young I was very naughty and lost 98% of my vision in my right eye and can only see out of it if I cover my other eye. I only wore glasses when I was in first grade and it broke right after first grade and I never got them again until my freshmen year. I have been to about eight different schools throughout my life and I have made very interesting friends in every single one of those schools. After my seventh grade year, my parents decided to move to California and try out if living over there was better than living here. The other reason for moving over to California is because both of my parents lived in California before coming to Minnesota and wanted to go back. My grades were very bad in middle school because I felt like I didn't really care back then. Now that I've reach high school it seems that I was really good at math and science, but I figured out that I was just very lazy during middle school. I also found out that I was very bad at learning literature for any language because I do poorly in Japanese and English class.

I was born before school started regularly, so I had to go to school late next year. Luckily, there was one school that started school on September 10th, so I attended that school with a two-hour bus drive away. We had to wake up 5:00am in the morning to get to the bus stop and I was still a kindergartener back then. That school just opened up and it had no playground to play, so we just played tag outside everyday. After completing that year, we moved to another school that was closer to us, so it would be easier. We didn't take the bus to that school but walked there. At that school I only had three Asian friends, two of them were twin brothers and they were Chinese. The other one was Hmong and he wasn't even in my class, but we knew each other through recess. Every year I had switched schools, sometimes even in the middle of the year.

My longest stay was in fourth grade where we stayed at the same school until I completed seventh grade.

During those four years I have participated in many of their celebrations. My favorite was Asian history month because we had a teacher that chose five students to do the dragon dance at the beginning which was really fun when we chose our role. People who were performing had exited to the back room, which was like a V.I.P zone, and where people rehearsed and made jokes. If I didn't perform, I was in the band section. Once I entered high school, they didn't put me in band and I was kind of sad, but not really because you had to come during zero period to practice in class. One of the interesting things about California was that lots of Hmong students couldn't speak or understand Hmong unlike here in Minnesota.

Sincerely,
Almost Lost My Vision

GRATEFUL MINNESOTA GAMER

Dear Teacher,
There are three things I wished you knew about me: I was in a serious car accident back in 2015, I like playing games a lot, and I went to visit my family in California over the summer and learned a lot of things from it. These are the things I wish you knew about me.

I was in a car accident back in 2015. It was when we came back from camping in Rochester, MN. The other car hit the back of the car, where my cousins and I sat. We were not wearing seat belts at the time because we were kids. My cousins both flew out the window, and I went into the back of the car. When I went to the hospital, they told me that I had an exploded spleen, two cuts on my head, and I may have had some bleeding in my brain. I was in recovery for a month, from what I remember. From what my siblings tell me, I have changed somehow.

Secondly, I wish you knew that playing games helps me release stress from things like school. When I have final exams, which is very stressful, playing games help me feel relaxed. Another reason is that I can make friends and learn some new things about life whenever I play games with or without other people. Also, it brings families together when playing outside games, like Mario Kart and a lot more.
When I went to meet family in California, it made me realize how much different my life could have been. If we did stay in California, I can imagine how tan I would be, and I wonder how little or big the house may have been. I even think about how my religion, friends, lifestyle could've been different. I wonder if I would have known Hmong, if I lived in California? Many things went through my mind while vacationing there.

I want you to know that I have been in an accident and it messed me up somehow. Playing games also help me release stress, make friends and learn new things. I went to California and that changed my mind about life. These are the things that I want my teacher to know about me.

Sincerely,
Grateful Minnesota Gamer

MIXED FEELINGS

Dear Teacher,

I'm a 14 years old girl who goes to Park Center. High school is not easy. Although many people say it's only 9th grade, it's pretty hard, but I have a lot of hopes and I will try my best to pass your class! I'm a very happy person. That is what people say to me. Sometimes people even tell me they want to be me because I'm always happy, but they don't know I can be sad sometimes. I don't really show my emotions to people. Not that I'm scared, but I just tell myself that it's going to be alright. I try to be positive. I spread positivity because sometimes people just need a little positivity in their life. Sometimes they didn't grow up like I did.

I have a mom and dad and also 4 siblings and a dog. Of course, people will se e that my life is complete, but like many families, my family has problems too. It's life and life will hit you a lot at some point. I see that a lot with my friends coming to school crying because of life. Wanting to kill themselves. Thinking that life is bad and that nothing good will happen. And I will be honest, I had thoughts in 4th grade. Even though I was still young I had feelings towards life. How I felt like and had the emotions to express it. Sometimes I cry because my parents will yell at me because my grades are bad. They even compare me to my brother. He was always the "A" student and a good student. Because of that, I thought I wasn't good enough. I wanted to be better. I didn't love myself. I wanted to make my parents happy, but I never really did. That was what I thought.

In fifth grade I started to notice things. How to love myself and accept who I was. Not a lot of people knew how to do that. The girls in my fifth grade class always complained about how ugly they were and how they can't do this and that. Sometimes I will just talk to them about you know, "love yourself" and "there is no one else like you." Some girls don't realize that they are enough. I think I realized that really early. I may be ugly to some people, but I don't care. I love myself.

In 6th and 7th grade, I had a hard time getting along with people. They treated me bad. Always starting drama with me, but I usually ignored it because some people are scared of me. I'm known for my strengths. I didn't really speak Hmong in middle school. Sometimes I forget I'm Hmong because I speak a lot of English.

During 6th and 7th grade my uncle, grandpa, and grandma all passed away so soon. I was very sad because they were like parents to me, especially my uncle, my dad's brother. He treated me like I was his daughter. He was like a dad to me. Hearing his tragic death, I cried and cried. I never got to say goodbye or an "I love you." It only felt like yesterday I was just talking to him. It's been 3 years now. I really miss him. My grandpa passed away next because of a heart attack. Later on, my grandma passed away not far from my grandpa's death. I knew she really missed him when he left. She called and called for him. She even cried because he never came. She was really old. And she didn't know that grandpa passed away. She would cry in her sleep. Why did she have to leave so soon, I thought. It's very lonely without them.

One year later, I transfer to a Hmong school, hoping for the best. It was the best choice I ever made in my whole life. I connected more, and I felt more comfortable. They understood me and knew where I was coming from. Sometimes we even cried together talking about life. They are my family, my brothers and sisters. We're Hmong. I feel stronger when I'm with them and they motivate me to do better. Although we go to different schools now, we check on each other and sometimes even meet and talk about life. I know we're only freshmen students, but sometimes I just need to check on people. I check on everyone. I check on my friends and family, other people I may or may not know, and even my enemies or people I dislike. I never hate someone because that is a strong word to say. Sometimes we just got to check on someone you know. Because just asking, "Are you okay?" may break them down. We all are human beings. Like I said before life brings you down. Sometimes I will just stop and ask people that question because I'm that type of person who doesn't want to see people sad. The reason why I am how I am is because of the people from the Hmong school and football. In the spring, I helped my teammates get better and helped them improve what they needed help on. I was the leader of that group. I carried the team. It was a great experience and a great honor to be in that team. A lot of teamwork and discipline.

Our next season, I will play for our school team. We had many small players and not very strong people, but we had a lot of hope. My coach had the people who he thinks are leaders come in a little meeting and talk about how to put the team together. I'm very grateful to have a person like him in my life. Because of him, I changed the way I am. I cared more about stuff around me and stayed more disciplined. My other coach he is very funny and understanding. I'm also grateful to have him in my life and being able to work together as a team. My third coach is a woman. One of my after-school teachers is very talented and unique. She sometimes talks to me about life and how I am doing in life. She is one of the reasons why I love the Hmong school. She is not Hmong and neither is my first coach. My second coach is Hmong. They are young teachers, maybe around their 20's. I'm very thankful for all the coaches! Volleyball coaches and football coaches. Right now, I'm feeling so many emotions writing this. It makes me remember about the feelings I had when I first entered the gym. So many nervous thoughts.

Who motivates me? Everyone one who looks up to me: my coaches, my friends and family, and my enemies or people I dislike. Nothing really stops me from reaching my goals. I learned how to keep moving on and I learned how to be me. Do what makes you happy and what makes you keep moving forward. I love everyone to be honest because anyone who comes in my life makes a difference. And I will never regret anything because if I did I wouldn't be here. Makes me love Hmong so much. I'm sad and happy right now because I miss my old school so much and the thought that I'm getting older. I'm a person that has mix feelings about things.

Love,
Mixed Feelings

❀+❀+❀+❀+❀+❀+❀+❀+❀+❀+❀+❀+❀+❀

MADE FUN OF ME

Dear Teacher,

I'm a sixteen-year-old junior student. I will be telling three things about me in this letter. First, I used to be very chubby and people would make fun of me, even my own dad. Second, I really enjoy playing soccer and other sports. Lastly, I don't really like to talk or do much, so expect me to be very lazy.

Back in elementary and middle school I used to be very big for my age because I was so lazy and never wanted to do anything, but play video games and eat. My peers would make fun of me because I was so slow during gym class or anything that involved movement. Even my dad would tell me that I need to stop eating so much and run. Whenever I finished a soccer game during the summer, he would always make me run another ten to twenty laps when we got home. When I got to middle school, I met a girl and we started to date, but broke up very quickly. My dad told me it was because I didn't look good since I was so chubby. After he told me that I started to workout everyday and lost weight. My dad was my inspiration because as soon as he and my mom started to go to the gym, I started to exercise with them.

Secondly, I started to play soccer at the age of six. Since my dad plays soccer, he and my mom signed me up for BPAA soccer. At first, I didn't really enjoy playing soccer since it would use up half of my summer and I would often miss going to my cousin's house due to practice or having a game. Also, because I would often get yelled at by my dad because I guess I wasn't running enough during the game. But as I got older I started to enjoy playing soccer more. I got to meet new people, see people from other schools that I didn't know played BPAA soccer too. The position I played was mostly defense and sometimes mid-field. Another sport I also enjoy playing is football. I started playing football because most of my cousins played it.

Lastly, I'm a very quiet student, and I don't really like to talk a lot. Growing up as a kid, my teachers would always tell me to speak up because I was too quiet. Everytime we had conferences in elementary school, my teachers would tell my parents that I didn't talk much at all. I just don't like to talk very much even with my friends. I'm the quietest out of all my friends, so expect me not to speak a lot in class, but I will try my best to talk more in class.

That is all I wanted to say in this letter. Thank you for reading it and I hope we get to know each other more.

Sincerely,
Made Fun of Me

BEHIND THE MASK

Dear Teacher,

When my parents named me, they wanted people to call me with my first and middle name together. I have gotten in trouble in the past for not telling my teachers to call me by my full name. So, call me by my full name, please. Just to tell you about myself, I have a lot of stress from time to time about things in life. I'm a bit insecure about myself and my future even though I'm doing well in school now. What worries me is when I reach college, I don't know if I will be able to do well. I'm scared of the future, like what I am going to do as a career, since I really don't have a job that will satisfy my parent. My parents are part of the reason why I have stress, but they are also the source of motivation I have for going through life. Stress is not the only mental health issue I have, I also have a bit of depression and anxiety, but I have ways to deal with these mental issues temporarily with music and gaming.

I really don't like my sister because she always has an attitude with my parents and the kids. She is always yelling everyday at the kids and sometimes my mom and dad. I would do something about it, but it will just cause more problem for my parent. My mom says that they got a handle on it. My sister is also a hypocrite and always has a excuse for everything even if she is wrong. When my parents ask her to watch the 2-year-old kid, she would be on her electronic devices watching stuff and not paying attention to him. I haven't talked to her since 6th grade because I don't want to. My brother's attitude is pretty bad too, but luckily it's not every day.

I don't think my dad would really care about my mental health issue because my parents went through more hardship than us. I don't really care if they understand me or this generation of hardships that we're going through now. I'm just so tired of being constantly reminded of life whenever I have fun. For example, like the other day I stayed for after school in the weight room and I had to call my dad to pick me up since the bus wasn't there that day. When he came to pick up me, we stopped at a red light and he asked me why I stayed after school and if that was going to help me for my future. I'm just so tired of it.

I have been down so much, but I keep moving forward. My friends tell me that I'm a smart person who is going to reach high, but they don't seem to notice this mask because this mask covers up everything. The mask is okay on the outside, but deep inside of me is just darkness covered by the light. The light is what I want people to see, but that darkness is still there as the shadow of the light. They don't seem to notice these chains behind me, and they don't see this is a one-way road that is not coming back. I'm not like this all the time, but at times where I am at my lowest.

I don't need help or any sympathy because it's already said and done, and it still affects me whether or not it's there. Like people who comes home after a war, the war might be gone, but the feeling and effect it has on you changes you forever, so you're not the same person. It might be the same thing we're going through as people, but there is really no way to get rid of it, unless you have no worries at all. I try my best, but it's not enough for my parents. Thanks for hearing me out. This has helped lessen the stress off of my chest.

Sincerely,
Behind the Mask

HLUB KOJ TUS KHEEJ

Nyob zoo Xibfwb,
Kuv xav kom koj paub txog kuv kev tsis tau paub hlub kuv tus kheej. Kuv tus phooj ywg hais rau kuv tias kuv muaj siab zoo thiab muaj zog rau tus kheej, tab sis kuv muaj ib tug kheej uas tsis ntseeg kuv. Kuv yeej tsis tau muaj kev txaus siab, hlub kuv tus kheej, thiab kuv yeej muaj kev ntxhov siab vim kev nyuaj siab xwb. Kuv tseem muaj siab loj thiab siab zoo tiam sis kuv tseem tsis tau ua zoo rau kuv tus kheej li. Kuv tsis xav pity rau kuv lub neej vim kuv paub tias kuv muaj zog txov kuv txoj siab.

Kuv nco qab thaum twg kuv yuav tawg, thiab tso kuv tus kheej, quaj quaj xwb. Kuv tsis zoo li cov ntxhais zoo nkauj, tsis muaj lub cev zoo, tso tseg vim cov ko kuv tsis zoo li co hluas nkauj. Thaum kuv loj hlob, kuv hais rau kuv tuj kheej hais tias, kuv yuav tsum muaj peev xwm, kuv lub neej yog kuv tau npaj, tsis yog lwm tus npaj, thiab kuv xav tau txoj kev ywj siab.

Kuv kev nyuaj siab tsis yog txog tsis zoo nkauj xwb tiam sis txog kuv tsev neeg dhau los cov teeb meem. Kuv nco qab thaum kuv tseem me me, kuv niam thiab txiv sib ceg txog nyiaj txiag, kev sib hlub txog peb, uas tsis tau zoo nraws li kev cai thiab txog peb cov neej. Kuv txiv siab luv thiab ntxub kuv niam, tiam sis kuv niam yeeb siab ntev u nus.

Thaum kuv tseem me me, kuv pom tus niam quaj' thiab nws lub siab ntsws lwj tag vim tsis muaj leej twg hlub nws, nrog nws, tuav nws thaum nws poob ntsej muag. Thaum kuv pom kuv niam zoo li ntawd, kuv tu siab heev thiab kuv yeej quaj nrog nws. Kuv xav tias kuv yauv tau ua ib yam dab tsi rau kuv niam, ua rau kom nws zoo siab thiab tsa nws tus ntsuj plig. Lub sijhawm ntawv, kuv niam thiab kuv txiv nyob ze rau qhov kev sib nrauj. Tu siab tshaj plaws thiab ua rau kuv thiab kuv plaub tus tij laug poob siab rau peb lub neej yam tom ntej. Tam sis no peb nyob laus lawm, kuv txiv thiab kuv niam ua zoo thiab si hlub ua neej lawm, tiam sis tseem muaj kev sib ceg me ntsis thiab. Tam sis no, kuv lub siab zoo lawm thiab kuv yuav tau hlub thiaj npaj kom tau kuv tus kheej kom zoo mus. Kuv yuav pab hlub thiab tso siab hlo rau kuv tsev neeg thaum peb nyob kev nyuaj siab. Tsis yog 'ua siab ntev,' tiam sis yog muaj zog thiab hlub koj tus kheej kom zoo.

Sau Npe,
Hlub Koj Tus Kheej

Family

Tsis Paub Kev Nyuaj Sab

Nyob Zoo Xibfwb,

Nyob zoo! Kuv muaj ntau yaam yuav lug qa txug kuv tug nkeej. Kuv tuaj txug rua teb chaws Mekas rau lub xyoo 2017. Kuv tug txiv ntxawm nrug rua nws ob tug tub tuaj tog kuv txiv wb tom tshav nyob hoom rau hauv Minnesota. Thaum kuv tuaj tau le ib lub hli ntau kuv nam hu tuaj nrug kuv tham; kuv nam noog kuv tas tau tuaj nyob rua teb chaws Mekas hab vaam meej lawm nwg zoo le caag hab puas xis nyob, puas muaj kev nyuaj sab dlaab tsis. Kuv tsis paub yuav teb le caag rua kuv nam, kuv tsuag has tas, yeej xis nyob kawg tabsis tau nyob huv tsev ntau xwb hos has txug kev nyuaj sab ces tsis muaj. Tabsis qhov tseeb kuv twb tsis paub tas kev nyuaj sab zoo le caag, hab yog dlaab tsis, lug txug rua tam sim nuav, kuv mam le paub tas kev nyuaj sab yog dlaab tsis. Nwg yog txhua yaam uas nyob rau yug lub neej tsis has qhov zoo losis yog qhov phem.

Kuv yog ib tug tib neeg tsis kheev tham lug ces zoo le kuv ca le zoo le ib tug neeg uas dub muag tabsis kuv yeej nyaam kev phooj kev ywg heev. kuv twb tuaj kawm ntawv huv lub tsev kawm Park Center tau ob xyoo tsua xyoo nuav lawm los kuv twb tsis muaj phooj ywg coob le tsuas yog muaj ob peb leeg xwb. Xyoo dhlau lug nua kuv txuj kev kawm ntawv nws tsis nyuaj luaj twg, tabsis lug tsua xyoo nuav kuv muaj ob lub hoob uas nwg nyuaj heev rua kuv, nws yog Science 9 hab English 9. Ob hoob nuav nwg nyuaj heev rua ntawm kuv. Txawm yuav nyuaj los kuv yuav ua kom tau tsaus le qhov kuv ua tau hab yuav rau sab kawm. Tsis tag le hov, yuav tsum xaav txug yug lub neej tom ntej hab yug lub hom phaj es yug haj le rau sab kawm hab xaav moog kawm ntawv. Kuv nam has rua kuv tas, yuav tsum xaav txug koj lub neej tom hauv ntej hab xaav txug koj tej menyuam, koj haj le rau sab kawm ntawv hab ua hauj lwm. Vim kuv nam hab txiv puab tsis tau kawm ntaub kawm ntawv haj yug tau peb lug txom nyem hab twb hlub tsis tau peb le qhov peb xaav tau. Yog le nuav, kuj yuav txum rau sab kawm ntawv hab le tau ua hawj lwm zoo, kuv haj le muaj nyaaj, haj le hlub tau kuv tej menyuam es tsis txhob ca puab txom nyem le kuv nam hab txiv. Tsis tag le, kuv yuav tau xaav tas tseem ntsuav kuv nam hab txiv nrug rua kuv cov nug muag uas tseem ua lub neej txom txom nyem nyob tim Nplog teb. Kuv tuaj rua teb chaws vaam meej lawm puab yeej tog tog kuv kawg le seb ho puaj muaj ib hnub kuv pab puas tau dlaab tsis rua puab has tas yog lawv tug ua tub los yog ua tij paab.

Ntawm kuv txuj kev kawm ntawv nwg nyuaj heev vim kuv tseem tsis tau paub lug mekas zoo, kuv haj le kawm ntawv nyuaj nyuaj ua rua kuv xaav tas sov kuv puas moog kawm ntawv qeb sab, txawm kuv yuav kawm tau zoo npaum twg los heev kawg seb kawm puas tag High School. Tabsis kuv muaj ib txuj kev xaav tas txawm nwg yuav nyuaj los yuav tau ua lub sab ntev kawm moog seb kawm puas tag 2 xyoo college. Kuv tug txiv kwj has rua kuv tas yuav tsum ua lub sab ntev hlo kawm moog kawm le kuv kawm tau tsuav moog kom taag 2 xyoo college thaum kuv moog nrhav hauj lwm ua haj le tau nyaaj ntau me ntsis yug kuv lub neej haj le tsis txom txom nyem heev.

Sau Npe,
Tsis Paub Kev Nyuaj Sab

Tsis Muaj Txiv Lawm

Nyob Zoo Xibfwb,

Thaum koj hais kom peb sau txog ib yam uas kuv xav kom kuv cov xibfwb paub ua rau kuv nyuaj siab vim kuv yeej muaj ib yav ua kuv xav txog xwb. Kuv yeej zoo siab thiab vim kuv tau sau txog qhov no rau koj nyeem.

Kuv xav kom koj paub hais tias kuv tsis muaj kuv txiv lawm. Kuv txiv tsis nrog kuv nyob lawm. Kuv txiv tau puv ib puas nees nkaum xyoo. Kuv txiv xiam vim rau qhov kuv txiv mob stroke. Kuv txiv xiam lub cuaj hli vas thib kaum yim xyoo 2015.

Muaj tej thaum muaj tej yam ua tau kuv nyuaj siab vim tsis muaj kuv txiv nyob nrog kuv lawm. Yog muab hais los kuv txiv yeej xiam tau ntev los lawm thiab. Tab sis zoo li kuv mus tsis txog qhov kuv txiv xav kom kuv mus txog. Yeej ua tau kuv nyuaj siab kawg vim kuv txiv yeej mob puag thaum kuv muaj peb xyoo lawm. Kuv yeej tsis tau pom saib kuv txiv lub neej zoo li cas thaum nws tseem ua neej nyob es tsis tau mob stroke. Kuv txiv yeej yog ib tug neeg ua kawm ntawv tau zoo heev li. Thaum nws tuaj txog teb chaws Mekas no, nws pib qib 9 txog qib 12. Nws cov hoob kawm yeej yog straight A xwb. Thaum nws kawm ntawv tas qib 12 nws yog tus thib ob hauv nws lub tsev kawm ntawv qib 9-12.

Kuv yeej xav kom kuv zoo ib yam li kuv txiv tab sis kuv lub hlwb khiav tsis zoo npaum kuv txiv lub. Kuv txiv yeej xav kom kuv mus kawm ntawv kom siab es thiaj li tsis txom nyem. Txij thaum kuv txiv xiam, kuv niam yeej ua hauj lwm sab kawg kiag. Kuv yeej tsis xav kom kuv niam mus ua hauj lwm li lawm. Tab sis kuv tij luag thiab kuv tsis tau mus ua hauj lwm ces tsis muaj leeg twg pab them nqi tsev nrog kuv tus tij laug hlob. Yeeb vim li ntawv, kuv thiaj xav mus kawm ntawv kom zoo es peb tsev neeg thiaj tsis txom nyem. Txawm kuv tsis keej thiab tsis paub npaum kuv txiv los kuv yeej yuav siv tas nrho kuv txoj kev xav kom kuv mus kawm ntawv tau siab. Kuv yeej yuav muab kev cia siab kom koj ho pab qhia kev kawm ntawv rau kuv.

Sau Npe,
Tsis Muaj Txiv Lawm

Mob Lub Siab

Nyob Zoo Xibfwb,
Kuv yog koj ib tug tub kawm ntawv. Yam kuv nyiam ua tshaj thaum tsis muaj dab tsi uas yog xyaum ntaus suab paj nruag xws li xyaum piano. Kuv nyiam siv kuv lub sij hawm seem nov los xyaum suab paj nruag vim hais tias kuv xav kom ib hnub tom ntej twg kuv yog ib tug tshaj lij ntaus piano. Tsis tas li ntawm kuv tseem nyiam kawm txog peb kab lib kev cai Hmoob. Kuv yeej tseem tsis tau nkag siab zoo zoo txog ntawm peb Hmoob kev coj noj coj ua hais tiag yog li cas tiag tiag. Kuv thiaj li xav muab kuv ib lub sij hawm seem coj los tshawb fawb txog peb Hmoob thiab.

Kuv muaj ib tus tij laug uas pab kuv thaum kuv nyuaj siab, thiab tsis tag li ntawv kuv tseem muaj tsib tug maum. Lawv pab kuv nrog kuv cov ntau ntawm thuam kuv xav tau kev pab. Hos kuv muaj ib tug niam tij, tsis tag li ntawv kuv muaj peb tug yawm yij uas hlub kuv thiab. Kuv txiv mus tham ib tug niam tshiab ces kuv txiv saib xyuas lawv tsev neeg es tsis saib xyuas peb lawm. Thaum kuv niam thiab txiv sib nrauj, kuv mob lub siab yog vim kuv txiv tsis nrog peb es mus nrog lawv lawm.
Hos kuv niam ces tham phone txog kuv txiv txoj kev phem tas li.

127

Thaum kuv hias dab tsis rau kuv niam ntawm kuv txiv ces kuv niam cav rov qab txog kuv txiv hias tias nws yog ib tug neeg phem. Muaj tej thaum kuv tsis niam nyob tsev vim kuv xav mus nyob tom tsev kawm ntawv vim hias tias tsis xav mloog kuv niam hias tej lus phem txog kuv txiv lub npe. Uas rau kuv tsis xav los tsev xav nrog phooj ywg nyob thiab tam txog kuv tej kev nyuaj siab xwb. Tam sim no peb nyob zoo thiab hos mauj tej thaum zoo li tsis xav nyob li. Yeej muaj tej thaum muaj kev sib cav sib ceg nyob rau hauv kuv lub tsev. Tsis tag li ntawv, thaum kuv niam thiab kuv txiv tseem hias plaub hias ntug, ua rau peb cov nus muag vwm tag li. Tus tug los tsis kam tham nrog kuv niam losis kuv txiv. Tam sim no ces thaum twg kuv niam thiab txiv sib pom ces sib cav kom ib tug muaj yeej muaj swb xwb. Kuv muab xav los yog vim li cas tej teb teeb meem hos los zoo li no. Thaum e peb nyob ib tse neeg uas tshaj lij heev thiab twb ntsawj txuag nyiaj ntswaj siv nyiaj. Tam sim no ces kuv tsev neeg twb tsis zoo li thaum e lawm os.

Sau Npe,
Mob Lub Siab

LESS WORDS AND EMOTIONS

Dear Teacher,
Being at Park Center for a year has opened my eyes to so many things and made me encounter many negative and positive obstacles. Knowing that you are a very open-minded and understanding teacher, I'm thankful

that you are willing to listen with an open heart, and willing to get to know what kind of world I live in.

The first thing that I wish you knew about me is that I come from a traditional Hmong family. My dad is a Mekong and a *Txiv Xaiv*, my mom is a Shaman, and my two younger brothers plays the qeej instruments. Therefore, my parents expect me to learn like the traditional Hmong girls. Growing up, I have been taught to cook, clean, babysit, and do well in school. My parents' expectations for me has always been set high, and I have always exceeded them. Throughout all my school years, I have always been that one student that receives A's in all my classes, and never went out with any of my friends. I have balanced my daily tasks of going to school, coming home and helping my dad prepare dinner, finishing my homework, and I started working soon after my Sophomore year. I always felt the need to find a job and help my mom pay for the bills, since my dad was unable to work due to severe back injury, and my sister was away for college.

Secondly, I wish you knew about my experience in Minnesota that shaped me to become the kind of person I am today. You may have known that my family has moved to many states and that I have only been in Minnesota for a year. Growing up, it has always been this pattern of going to a new school, making new friends, becoming adjusted, and leaving my friends. As you may have noticed, I'm always a quiet student in your class. I think it's obvious though, that it's not only your class that I'm quiet in. Throughout school days, I'm either never speaking or rarely speaking. I was never the quiet student until I moved to Minnesota. I also never disliked school as much until Minnesota. Before coming to Park Center, I attended another MN high school because my family was living with my uncle at that time. Going to that school, I never felt like I belonged there, and never felt that it was a place I was welcomed to. Going to school was a thought that I dreaded, because I wasn't looking forward to anything. I always saw other students cheerfully talking to their friends, which made me miss everything and everyone from my previous school. I felt that I didn't have anyone to express or vent to. My best friends were thousands of miles away, and they couldn't cheer me up physically. After facing all those problems, I became a person of less words and emotion. Although some things haven't changed, as of now, I'm just working towards graduation.

The last thing that I wish you knew about me is that I used to play the violin. Back in my elementary years, I had this passion of playing that instrument, and I'm thinking about getting back into it. I feel that by playing an instrument, It will help me cope with stress and problems that I face. Back when I played the violin, I was always dedicated and did an exceptional job in playing it. However, after transferring schools, I didn't have the class that I needed to continue improving my skills. Now that I'm at an older age, I feel that I could go back and advance in my skills.

Everything has been a mixed blessing, but I'm extremely grateful to know that you are interested in listening to my personal story. Although I'm the student that keeps my thoughts, and comments to myself, I'm able to smile and laugh more when I'm in your class. Simply, because you create a joyful atmosphere and you are willing to embrace everyone for who they are. I hope that after hearing my story, you can be someone I will continue to express and talk to when I need someone to listen.

Sincerely,
Less Words and Emotions

SUPPORT FOR ME

Dear Teacher,

I have always been that one Hmong American student that would work alone and independently. As you noticed, I have been learning Hmong from you for two years. I have always been the student who really didn't communicate with my classmates ever since transferring to this school. You were the teacher who inspired me to want to become a Hmong World Language teacher because of what is happening to our Hmong culture in this 21st century. I'm pretty sure that you would always wonder, "Why does he always complete assignments that I haven't even assigned to my students?" There are many things that you have known about me at school. However, there are many experiences and obstacles that I faced that even you don't know about that I went through to be able to get where I am today. I have been dying to tell you about three things but didn't have the words to say until now.

First of all, I have always been on the go when it comes to learning in school and living in one place. I have moved from many different states at different times, which impacted me a lot. My family and I have moved from Michigan to Wisconsin, North Carolina to California, and finally California to Minnesota. Whenever I transfer to a new school, I always fear that I would be moving soon, which causes me to not make any friends for I know that it's very painful and sorrowful to leave your best friends behind. I know that my friends will miss me dearly and I will miss them. I have that mindset that if I stay as an introverted learner and do things by myself, I wouldn't have to feel the same pain when leaving my loved ones behind. Sadness is like a drug to me, it takes me away from reality. It makes me see and think about the whole world differently. Thus, I must not create anymore sadness to others and myself when departing.

Secondly, you might have known that I'm the oldest son in my family, but my story doesn't just end here. Being born as the oldest son in a Hmong family puts me in a tight spot. According to Hmong culture, the oldest son is the one who carries on the Hmong traditions in a family. My parents were both born in Laos and have very high expectations for me not only to get a job with a good salary, but to continue the ways of the Hmong culture in America. I know that both of my parents really care for me and just want me to be successful, but their expectations are what is holding me back in life. I live in two completely different worlds: 1) Living as a Hmong child and learning all about the culture and traditions, and 2) Living as an American child whose dream is to become a teacher and contribute to society. From a young age, my father would sing the words of a *Txiv Xaiv,* a man who gives life lessons or precious golden words for children at funerals to live a good life after the death of a family member. He would always sing and use a microphone to help him memorize the significant words. My father would always tell me that I need to learn about Hmong culture, so that I can sustain a good life. He would always tell me his story of how he was disrespected by Hmong elders for not knowing anything about his culture at his younger age. Therefore, he decided to make me learn about our own culture and traditions, so that our family can be respected and acknowledged by other families. My father doesn't want me to face those kinds of negativity when I grow up to start my own family.

For the Hmong people, pride is very important for the husband of the household. Starting that day, my dad would take me to learn how to blow the *qeej,* a bamboo instrument that is used in Hmong funerals to help guide the dead to the afterlife. Even today, my parents encourage me to learn more about Hmong culture. Almost every day I would always be stressed out to continue to learn the old Hmong ways of life and learn the new American ways of life too. In my mind, I would always be confused and stressed about which world I truly live in as I stand between the boundary of Hmong and American culture. No one truly understands my confusion and what went through my mind. I'm hoping that my story will give you an idea of what I felt about being a Hmong American son.

Lastly, as a Hmong child growing up, I have faced many negativities that pulled me down at times. Throughout my childhood, other people laughed and made fun of who I was. I was judged for being Hmong-American. I was judged for being short and small. I was judged for who I am. Many of these painful words would gush through my head and fill me up with sadness. But I kept telling myself to stay strong, yet I didn't know how. Day by day, I would try to stay strong and would hide my true feelings. I had so many things that I wanted to say, but I just couldn't let it out. My mouth stayed silent as the inside of me wanted to scream out all my feelings that I have been storing inside my head, yet the only thing that came out of my mouth was…nothing.

When my family and friends would ask me if I was doing alright, all I could say was "I'm okay," all while trying to show a smile. Words are more painful than a knife stabbing my heart. Do you know why? A knife can be taken out, but painful words will always stay in your heart never leaving you. Painful words will always show me the past of how powerless I was. I'm standing all alone while society is quickly changing. My true self hidden within me is slowly fading away. No one is there for me when I'm there for them. If my friends were to have sad thoughts and wanted to jump off a bridge, I wouldn't jump with them. Instead, I would be at the bottom ready to catch them with my two hands. I have tried over and over to face these words throughout my whole entire life. By being in a lot of pain, I try to cover up my pain from everyone else. As I continue to walk my own path, I continue to face these negative thoughts and feelings that would try to blind me from my own future. These words of prejudice, discrimination, and unfairness would slowly drag me down to the depths of darkness. Yet I try my hardest and best to not let those words change what I see in my path. Today, I have gotten much stronger and more confident in my abilities. Those painful words will start to fuel up the fire within me and make me more confident.

I wish you knew about what I faced in life because what I needed most was support, someone to hear about my story, someone to know about my story, and someone with a helping hand when I'm stumbling. I wanted to tell you that your acts of kindness have helped me find out what I want to be in the future. Along the way, I know I will need your guidance and assistance to help me. I want you to know what life changing events occured in my life, that made me who I am together. I am and will always be the Hmong-American student who works silently and independently.

Sincerely,
Support for Me

JUST WANT A PERFECT FAMILY

Dear Teacher,
This is my first year having you as a teacher and it's so wonderful to share a little bit of me and my family with an adult who is willing to take their time to listen and read this letter. Thank you. Here is what I would like

you to know about me and my family.

My father is not really in the picture as much. What I mean is he only comes to my house every other day when he has the time. On the other days, he goes to his other house, the house that he lives in with his first wife. Some days he doesn't go to the other house either because he owns a farm and is really dedicated to it. My father would go to work in the cities and then right after work, he would go to his farm and spend his nights and days there. He doesn't really help a lot with my mom and us because he is always busy, but sometimes he will help out with money, if me and my sister really need help. For example, when school is about to start he will usually give me and my sister some money for school supplies or other things we might need. Since my mom is the second wife, she tends to tell us that my father doesn't love her as much as the first wife, for my father doesn't love me nor my sister as much. There have been times when they get into bad arguments and my sister and I can't do anything about it, so we will sit in our room and cry silently without them knowing because we both want a perfect family with a mom and a dad.

My father is a typical Hmong guy, who has two wives, but still talks to other women. My father got in trouble with my mom and my step-mom because of his actions. They were both really mad and upset at him because of the horrible, dirty actions that he has done. That was when I lost hope in a perfect family. My mom was really sad and broken hearted that after the incident she asked me and my sister if they should get a divorce and my older sister said, "Do whatever makes you happy, we will support you. If you are not happy with dad, don't let us hold you back." I also said the same thing, but on the inside, I wanted to say "NO! Please don't," because I didn't want to lose either one of them; I was so broken-hearted on the inside.

When that incident took place, I would cry everyday because I was so sad and couldn't hold it in. My sister was also breaking on the inside, and she would cry too, but hardly let on because she wanted to be strong for the both of us. Some people, like my father, will just never learn from their mistakes.

My mom basically raised me and my sister without a man in her life and I respect that very much because she is a strong, independent woman, and I love her so much. This is what I would like you to know about my education and school life. I like school, but when it becomes hard, I become really stressed and overthink many things. Even when I'm not stressing out, I still overthink many things like "Am I good enough? Am I smart enough? I'm going to fail." When I'm stressed, I don't really like to let people know or I don't like expressing it as much. I also have performance anxiety, meaning that I can't present or perform for a large audience, or even a classroom size. My performance anxiety is not really a big issue because it only happens once in a while. Some signs of performance anxiety for me are paleness, quietness, shaking or shivering, not making eye contact with anyone, my vision becoming blurry, and my eyes watering up. Afterwards I will usually cry and my heart will race super fast.

I have a goal of becoming a doctor, either a neurosurgeon or a pediatrician. My high school goals are to have good grades, A's the highest and B's the lowest. Also, with those grades I want to graduate high school and go to college for my doctorate degree.

In the future I do and don't want to get married. If I take the time to study and become a doctor, I don't think I would have time to be in a relationship; I don't want to get distracted. I do want to have kids of my own, but at the same time I want to adopt a child from either here in the United States or overseas because I want them to grow up how I did with a roof over my head, food to eat, clothes to wear, and most importantly a parent who loves them. Thank you again for giving me this opportunity to speak of the things that are on my mind and that affect me emotionally and mentally. This opportunity means a lot; thanks for listening.

Sincerely,
Just Want a Perfect Family

UNDER SOMEONE'S SHADOW

Dear Teacher,

I want you to know that I had an older sister, a year older than me. She had asthma and passed away from her first asthma attack. I was at the age of 7 or 8. I'm not afraid to tell what happened, because I understand that when I'm curious of how something happened, you would be curious too. I remember it was some time in December. My older sister, my mom, and I were going to one of my aunt's Hmong wedding. It was at 6:00 in the morning when we woke up and everything happened so quickly the following hour.

My older sister was taking a shower and I was in the kitchen, snacking on something. When she got out of the shower, she was screaming "PAB KUV OS, PAB KUV OS!" She couldn't breathe. My mom rushed to see what's going on and took my sister to do her nebulizer. She felt better after, but still had a difficult time breathing.

A few moments later she put on her clothes and then she fell down the stairs screaming for help again. My sister turned pale, then purple; she couldn't breathe. My mom told me to hurry up and get the inhaler. I grabbed it really quick from upstairs and rushed to give it to my mom. It didn't work. My mom and I were in tears, screaming, begging my sister to wake up. My other two siblings were sitting on the couch not knowing what to do or how to react, they were in shock, I guess. My mom was a nurse, so she tried CPR on my sister, but it didn't work. She called the cops, then called my dad. I just sat and watched, I couldn't do a thing. My dad came before the cops and he burned the xyab, a fragrant incense, trying to see if our ancestors could help my sister.

Help finally came: three cop cars, two fire trucks, and one ambulance outside my house. They tried CPR on her again, but it didn't work. Then they put her on the bed. My mom told me to watch my siblings and that my grandpa was going to pick us up. She called my grandpa to pick me up and my siblings. My mom and dad left in the ambulance with my older sister. When me and my siblings were at my grandma's house, my baby aunty asked me why I was crying so much, and I told her everything. My baby aunty and I were close, because we were only a couple months apart in age. So, we were on the floor crying, wishing my sister wouldn't die, and hugging each other. We both cried for an hour or two. Then, we stopped, hoping my sister survived, until my other aunty (my baby aunty's sister), was on the phone crying. I didn't think anything was wrong with my sister, so I asked her if her boyfriend broke up with her or something. She didn't answer me back. When she got off the phone, she told me that my older sister passed away. That was when I started breaking down again and it got even worse. My baby aunty and I cried longer on the floor; we both didn't want to do anything.

It was the funeral. I didn't have an appetite, neither did my baby aunty. Everything we ate tasted nasty. I saw my sister's face in her casket all quiet and asleep. I tried to stay away so I wouldn't cry in front of everybody. I was really heart broken, but as a kid everything was all about fun so that saved me from my sorrows and stress.

My mom had anxiety, and she had to take pills to make her feel better. She had been through so much and had a lot of stress. We didn't have any more money, so we had to start over on everything. We began saving again. Although I didn't get the things I wanted, I never complained. I didn't have to go to school for like four weeks and, when I got to school I had so many things to catch up on. I had so many papers inside my desk and, I was only a 3rd grader at that time. My teacher didn't seem to like me because, when someone was gone she never assigned them work but me. I was going through a lot as a young child, and she gave me all the papers I had to do for all the weeks I missed. It made me feel left behind, uncomfortable, and embarrassed. If only I knew she treated me differently from the rest of the kids, I would have stood up for myself. I didn't realize she was treating me differently until middle school started.

All this stuff changed me as a person. I was once a follower, listening to people's orders, depending on other people, and just doing what the other kids did. I was always under someone's shadow, until my sister died. I knew I had to change my ways. I became an independent person. I always depended on myself, and people depended on me. I started to learn to stand up for myself, to become more confident, and to be clear about what I wanted to say.

My parents would always tell me how I was so much better before my older sister passed away because I was quiet and never bothered to play with kids. I only did that because they told me to. My parents taught me to become someone who is quiet and dependent on others. I changed for the better. I don't regret acting how I acted now. I just changed into a whole different person, because of stress. Because of the way I act or my new personality, I don't feel like everything's a competition and that I always have to be the best, so someone looks at me in a different way. People will always have something to say, or always need to say their "opinion." I'm living my best life and I made it through my accomplishments and dreams. I don't do it so people will see I have a good life. I do it for my parents, myself, and my next generation.

Sincerely,
Under Someone's Shadow

❀+❀+❀+❀+❀+❀+❀+❀+❀+❀+❀+❀+❀+❀

WISH I COULD TURN BACK TIME

Dear Teacher,
It has been awhile since I have learned Hmong in school. The last time I learned Hmong was in second grade, at a local Hmong charter school. It's going to be a new learning experience for me again. Anyways, I'm a senior this year and I think there are going to be many transforming emotions throughout the years, but I'm willing to always do my best at school, home, and work.

It's a new school year and it has only been about 3 years since I have been here. I came during sophomore year and honestly it was really hard making friends. I was unable to make friends until I reached my junior year. I had my sister during my second year at high school and I would always hang out around her. I was super awkward, quiet, and shy. I hated doing group projects because I didn't know anyone. I didn't like being shy because it was a struggle to make friends and I would usually sit by myself during lunch until junior year.

In my sophomore year, I had a "friend" who I had class with, her name was Callie. She introduced me to a few of her friends, but I didn't feel connected with them, so I stopped hanging out with them. That was a hard decision because it was my chance to make friends, but I threw it out because of feeling uncomfortable. I went and stayed with my sister and her group of friends. I still felt uncomfortable being around anyone and I tried and think positive saying, "I hope I will be able to make friends that I could be myself around." For junior year, the first week I was alone again. I really didn't want to be alone this year so I couraged up and ask this one girl if I could sit with her and her name was Paj. I became super close with her and "our" friends now. I was glad to have made a move and I'm feeling better than ever.

For my personal life, it was difficult and complicated, and I wish I could turn back time to when I did something that was wrong. I was eleven at the time and my mom got remarried. My father died when I was about five years old and it was a struggle getting through without him because we were all emotionally depressed and mourning for the lost of our father. I have 11 siblings including me and not all of them are blood related to me. My mom had 3 husbands in total and the first resulted in 7 of my siblings. The second husband was my dad and they had 4 children total. Lastly, she met her third husband, who I don't know well, but he had kids of his own. I have half siblings and step-sisters and brothers. My family is really big thinking about it, but that is the fun of it. Back to when my dad died, when I went back to school, I was bullied for not having a dad and that was sad. They laughed at me cause my dad died and just said really negative stuff that I couldn't tolerate. I only had one friend who was by my side during that time and that was PaSee. I knew her since 1st grade, but unfortunately, I had to move away because my sister wanted me to learn english. I was separated from my mom to go live with my sister for better. I went to elementary school and it was a new experience for me to make friends. As I start to know people and become friends with them, I felt comfortable. Having recess and playing four square was the best.

As for work, it's been a year since I started working and I really enjoy it. I work at a nursing home where I serve them their food. Some residents are very cranky, and it's sometimes hard to cope with them, but there are some that are very gentle and nice. Overall, they are old, and I understand where they're coming from, so I'm more polite towards them. There are days where I am super exhausted after school and just want to go home and knock out, but can't because of work. The people at my workplace are very loving, caring, and very entertaining. There is never a day where I find it boring, it might be tiring, but afterward it's relaxing and enjoyable to talk to people about daily life and stuff. We're all friends and we always hang out after work, go to Tii Cup and enjoy some boba drinks, eat out, or just hang out at someone's place. I love the environment there, the food, and the people. I couldn't have found a better workplace.

My school life, personal life, and work life has had such a big impact on me. I wish I could have turn back time to days where I did something wrong and fix them, but I have learned that I can never go back and to just keep on going and make things better than what they use to be.

Sincerely,
Wish I Could Turn Back Time

INTERRACIAL DATING

Dear Teacher,

I was born into a family with already 8 children. Everybody was two years apart, except for my younger sister and me. Three weeks after my birth, my paternal grandpa died, and then in 2005 my family moved from Thailand to the United States.

When I started 11th grade I met my boyfriend through a friend of mine. We texted a little bit before homecoming. On the day of the homecoming both of our dates stood us up. So, we decided that we were going together. That night after the dance, his friend messaged me and told me that we looked good together and my date really liked me. I told him he was mine that night, we have been dating for almost a year now. Our relationship did have some problems. Everyday my parents would always tell me to dump him, for they didn't approve of a black guy being my lover. His friends would tell him that it was a bad decision because there was another girl who liked him, and they knew each other better.

The reason why my parents wouldn't let me date a black guy wasn't just because they were racist. My sister had married a different race and her life didn't end up as well as she has thought. Her husband didn't even pay for the bride price that my parents had asked of him. After two years of having their first son, her husband forced her out and was seeing another woman. My sister knew that that was the reason he was chasing her out. She came to live with us with her son. Less than a year after, her husband came back and begged her to go and live with him again. My parents wouldn't let her go, so she secretly took a cab to the airport and went to live in Massachusetts. When she was pregnant with her second son, her husband told her to get out of his house three times a day. When her son was born they got divorced and my sister moved back to live with us. After about a year her ex-husband then sold the house and came to live with us. He also disrespected my parents and argued with them saying that they were stupid.

I believe that because of what had happened recently between my sister and her ex-husband, my parents highly disapproved of the idea of interracial dating and marriage. They fear that one day I might be in the same situation as my sister. I just wish that they would support me and my relationship. I know it's hard for them to accept the fact that I'm dating a black guy because of what one of their daughters has gone through. At the same time, I'm always thinking if the guy I'm in a relationship with is really worth it. Is he worth the arguments I have with my parents?

When I think about the things that I want to pursue in life, the things that I love to do, there is always someone to stop me from doing it. When I was in a dance group, I asked my father to take me to practice. He would always tell me no. He would give me a lecture of how dancing was bad, a waste of time and if it wasn't for serving god then don't do it. In middle school, I would go to volleyball practice and we would finish late. Whenever my dad came and picked me up, he would tell me to stop going because nobody wanted to pick me up. When I was in orchestra and brought my instrument home to practice my dad would tell me "stop bringing that trash home, it's noisy." I quit orchestra the year after. When I had a performance or a concert, my parents wouldn't appear. I would always give the excuse that they were busy with the garden or with my little nieces and nephews. That is all I wanted to share with you.

Love,
Interracial Dating

I Would Have Turned Out Differently

Dear Teacher,

I'm just one of your many students, the one who doesn't stand out, but is a very introverted and quiet. I always try my best at school, but I always struggle here and there; someone who is too shy to ask for help sometimes. In my household I'm the oldest child, so there is not anyone to lean on and depend on to help me with school work when I need help. Sometimes I ask my friends for help, but I don't want to be a bother so most of the time I work on it until I understand. I always get frustrated, but when I finally understand I feel happy and proud of myself. Both my parents expect me to get all As and when I do, it makes my mom proud which makes me happy about my accomplishments.

My parents divorced when I was 11, and my dad was no longer in my life when I was 12. Throughout most of my life, my family had many negative moments and I can't remember any really good memories of my parents being happy together. I never really noticed that it wasn't normal because I was too young to understand at the time. My dad would still be in my life right now if he didn't cheat or made other bad decisions. Or at least things would have turned out differently. For around the 6 months that my dad was still in my life after my parents divorced, I was very mad at him and didn't want to be with him because I couldn't accept all the changes that happened in my family's lives when he decided to marry a young woman from Loas. However, my dad ended up making another mistake that made a big change in my sibling's and my life, where he suddenly wasn't a part of our lives no more. I thought I was okay with it, but I didn't realize how I felt deep down at the time and never knew it would affect me so deeply to the point where it would change my attitude.

I rebelled against my mom and never listened to her or my step-dad. I never got along with my family for around the first a year and a half without my dad in my life. I would always argue with my mom and step-dad, and it affected both my mom and I deeply. My step-dad always has said hurtful things to me and would always bring up my dad. It would bring up my anger more, and to this day my step-father and I are still not on good terms. My step-dad left for around two years and recently came back last year. During that time my family and I have spent time together and are closer now. Sometimes, no longer having my dad in my life is hard, and my little siblings don't remember much about my dad and think he is a bad person who left us from what my mom and step-dad tell them. After all, I'm glad my parents are no longer together because my mom is very happy now.

I remembered when I was younger and one day I was talking to my dad. He told me that kids who grow up without a father figure will more likely not be successful. I didn't agree with him, nor did I want to believe him. My dad was always very negative, and I never realized until I got older and I would think of the old memories that I would remember. I try very hard to do well in school, so I can prove my dad wrong and show that I can be successful. My family wants me to go to college and get my master's degree. A couple of my aunties have got their master's degree, and my grandpa really wants me to graduate with my master's degree, so I will work hard to get it.

The main reason I signed up for Hmong class was because I wanted to understand and learn how to speak our language as well as the culture. My family is very Americanized, so we don't speak Hmong at home. My Hmong is not very good, so I can not read hmong or pronounce most of the words correctly. However, I wish to improve and will try my best and learn in your class, even though things will be very challenging for me. Something I want to change about Hmong parents is to believe in their kids and to not underestimate them. I hope that Hmong parents will be more supportive towards their kids and let them be. To let them grow up doing what they wish to do for their future or job.

Thank you,
I Would Have Turned Out Differently

I Just Want to Give Up and Never Try

Dear Teacher,

I'm a freshman this year. I live with my family. I have a sister, but she doesn't take Hmong class. I have an older brother who is in college right now, but he still lives with us. My mom and dad are still married both working part-time jobs during the day. We never have breakfast together in the morning because not everyone is at home. My mom is already off at work, my brother is at college, and me and my sister have to get ready for school and our bus comes early too. My dad usually stays home till noon then he leaves for work. However, we would never miss dinner.

My mom and dad want my siblings and I to become very successful in life; they want the best for us, but they don't make it easy. Sometimes when they tell me to do good in school and I end up not doing well, and they get very upset and lose all faith in me. The harder I try to do better, the more I end up doing worse. They think that it's hopeless to hope for their children, especially me, to do good in the future and I would really appreciate if they had some faith in me for once.

When I'm at school, sometimes I just want to give up and and never try. The pressure and stress that I have at home and school are so frustrating; it gets me very emotional. Sometimes I just want to go to my bed and scream my head off and not stop till I was done, which was never. I knew I had to keep going, and I know that I'm never going anywhere if I don't do anything about it. I know that even if I tell my parents this, they will never understand how much stress and frustration that goes through my head and think that I'm just lazy. I always think to myself that nobody is going to ever understand how you feel even if you tell them with your own words. I try to just deal with this and act like it's nothing, but it's always gonna be a something. Now obviously my parents would never want to put me through this kind of situation, but sometimes they push me too far over the edge that it causes me to react like this. I wish I could be like the kids who can do their homework and assignments without any problems. I wish I can be those kids who get straight A's and who are always known as the "smart" ones.

Homework can be a pain at times. When it's too much, and I can't seem to figure it out, I always have the mind-set that thinks, "I can't do it" "I'm gonna get a bad grade on this assignment" and the worst, "I'm gonna fail this class." Some of the classes that I take I actually enjoy. Some others I would say "why did I even sign up?" But I don't want to be a drop-out, nor do I want to be a quitter. I want to keep going strong and I don't want to stop and keep going, but I have to admit, there are a lot of hardships and obstacles that I have to go through that will bring me to the decision to give up. However, I will not back down, hopefully. I want to get good grades in all of my classes. I want to be that straight A student, the kid that comes home with their report card and their parents don't have to worry about it because they know they have already had good grades. I want to be the best for myself. I want to graduate for god sakes!

Sometimes I think that my family always wants me to uphold a stereotype. Not just any stereotype, the typical Asian stereotype. Where Asian kids supposedly get straight A's and great test scores. They get one problem wrong on their math test. Their teacher loves them because they are the smartest in the class. Everyone wants to copy off homework from them because they have all the correct answers. Their report card has no flaws and good notes from all teachers. The kids that have a great future in front of them. Well that is not me. I don't think that will ever be me, but I think that it's okay. It's fine not to be the greatest student in the entire school, class, or grade because not everyone is great. Not everyone is amazing, and I'm not great, I'm not amazing. I'm just me.

Aside from this, there are other things I would like you to know. For starters I'm not the type of person who is very outgoing and open towards new people. If there is a time where we sit and talk to the people around us and I'm surrounded by random people, don't expect me to be starting a long conversation with everyone. What teachers don't understand is that I feel very uncomfortable talking to others who I am not familiar with, especially when the teachers force us to talk to each other. I understand that they want us to communicate with one another and try to be nice to each other, and most importantly become friends with one another, but not everyone is going to do what the teacher asks of and not everyone is going to like you. I know it's very selfish and a bit rude of me to say but this is a dear teacher letter.

Sincerely,
I Just Want to Give Up and Never Try

JUST LOVE ME UNCONDITIONALLY

Dear Teacher,

I just wanted to tell you that it's hard for me everyday in school because of anxiety and other things in my thoughts. My attention span is focused 50% of the time, but I still managed to get through the day with a certain amount of effort at the end of the day. One thing that motivates me is something I'm really unsure of. Life hits everyone, but I feel so overwhelmed and stressed about it every second to minute to hour and day of my life as if I was going through more than anyone else. What brings me down comes from my own effort and relationships. I have been going through the same pain mentally these past few months and years and I realized most of my pain would come from just the people I love unconditionally. However, what makes me fight still today is something that I can't tell. It feels as if a person left its shell and all you really see is the outside of that person. Until you see how the inside is, it's empty. I'm the only 1 son out of 4 sisters and I live with both of my parents. You know I don't really wish for more than what I have, but to only strive further into life. My experiences that I have had, especially from my family and personally during the summer and every past year until today, was rough.

Being the only son we all know that is tough. What is even tougher are parents who don't understand you. It's the worst thing a kid can have in life. Even if one parent was more modern and understanding enough to agree with the things I do and the actions I take, it's just not always shown in the words they say. It's hard because I can rarely go out with friends or girlfriends who are not part of the family, even though my mom is usually an understanding parent from time to time. Yes, of course I'm the only son, Yes, of course they want me to do great in life. Yes, of course they just don't want to see me following their paths. Regardless of that, I have been taught that parents will never see the good in you and the changes in you. No matter how old you are.

To me it feels as if I make one little mistake, and I'm not mature. It's like I don't do one thing, and they take my freedom away from me and "LOVE" to see me suffer. You see, many people would just be rebellious and do what they love, which is great. But I no longer sometime understand my parents nowadays. In fact, not to be disgraceful, but I hate the tradition in Hmong culture sometimes. It doesn't suit how I live my life, but I respect it. You see, I'm the only son and I have seen so much in life at this age and done so much. Even my maternal uncles and aunts question me, "why do you live and act as if you are in your 30's? Why not go enjoy life and live as a teenager?"

Apparently, I have gone through a lot like family violence, family issues, family problems, relationship issues, depression, arguing, crying, and all the above you can say. What my parents don't understand is that I can live up to my own responsibility and be a man of my own when it comes to being responsible outside of the house. I don't think they will ever understand how much of a changed person I am and how much I have grown today. That is why they don't rely on me doing much of the things I love. I don't understand when they will ever see me as a changed man. It's hard because they still treat me like a child, but what is even more sad is having parents who just wouldn't understand your perspective and your emotions. I don't know what to say much, but this is part of something in my life that brings me down to the bottom of earth all the time.

I sometime don't know why I'm still living carrying all these memories and sadness in me. My observations and being mentally hurt made me who I am. This is what brings me down the most. I just wish that I can live my life after highschool and college is over. I just want to live freely without any restrictions under anyone and be able to breathe instead of always letting my internal thoughts eat me day by day. I just wish for myself to be greater than the last generations, but I also wish everyone in my family changed as well too. Overall, I just wish for all parents to be understanding even if you are strict, you need to have a big heart too, because everyone has to learn in life in order to grow and be successful from the mistakes they make.

Sincerely,
Just Love Me Unconditionally

THANK GOD SHE COULD SPEAK ENGLISH

Dear Teacher,

I have been keeping these secrets away for over 5 years, and I think this would be a great time for me to finally let it out for people like you to know. I would like someone like you to listen to my story, my hardships, the goods and bads throughout my life, because I trust you. I want you as a teacher to know the life that I have blocked people from viewing.

Throughout my life in elementary school I had always been quiet, my classmates would always ask me why I was so quiet? Why don't I talk? Do I not know how to talk? I will always remember that moment when I first spoke in class for everyone to hear. Their eyes widened as if they were seeing a trash can talk for the first time. Despite being the only Asian in that class, what hurt me the most was after I presented my paper, I heard a white boy said, "Thank god she could speak English." But being as quiet as I am, I couldn't do or say anything, but inside I was boiling. In my mind, I would shout as many bad words in Hmong at him; it wasn't effective at all because he didn't know what I was thinking.

Those kids were not the only problems I had because our neighbors were the same. They would sometimes shout racist stereotypes like, "Yellow skins are living next to us." My parents didn't know much English, so they would smile and wave at them, not knowing what they were saying. It felt as if they were watching me and my family's every wrong move. Everything we did was wrong to them. I wanted to protect my parents from them because they are rude people, but what could a little 4th grader do? My blood boils every single time they gave that look to us; it made me just want to shout the meanest thing that I could think of. Some days I would wish all people around me would just disappear, so that I didn't have to deal with racism any more.

The second thing I want you to know is that my parents split-up 2 days right before I started my first day of middle school. The first day of middle school made me stressed out a lot, but my parents' divorce just stressed me out even more. I had so many thoughts going around in my mind that brought me back to the day my mom asked my siblings and I, "Who would you choose to go with if your dad and me split?" She was giving us a hint all this time, but I didn't want to choose; I didn't want to be a child who has only one parent, and I didn't want the word "step" in my family. I went to school the following next two days. Any kid would feel nervous if they were in my shoes, but I wasn't nervous, nor was I feeling excited either. I felt as if I was just empty, like a human with no emotions; I felt lost, as if I didn't have both parents then I would rather be an orphan with no parents. Many thoughts passed through my mind all day to the point where I felt like giving up. I felt as if I couldn't continue my life anymore; everything had shattered. At the end of the day, I come back home to an empty house that was once filled with beautiful memories and pictures that had bad editing but was lovely to look at.

I missed the old days before none of this ever even happened. I went to visit my dad after a week passed by hoping for my parents to be back together; I even missed a school day, but school didn't matter to me anymore. All I cared for was to see my father after two, long days without him. Although I never got to know what happened or why my parents split, most nights I would hear them argue, but I didn't think much about it. I thought it was just an argument about money and that was it until I heard my mom talking to my grandma about my dad cheating on her at work with another woman. My hope for my parents to get back together faded. Is he going to marry her? Am I going to have step-siblings? These questions filled my mind, as I couldn't imagine myself with a step-mom and step-siblings. I didn't want my dad to be somebody else's biological father because there will be me and my siblings left with no father to claim.

Towards the middle of the school year, it had been several months since I last visited him, and I still didn't want to see him either. I rode the bus home from school like always. A few minutes of walking before I got home, about a block more, something caught my eyes in the distance where I stood. It was my aunt waving at me. It made me wonder why was she here. I went inside to find my dad with my mom sitting on the table discussing their divorce. I then started to have a little hope jumping somewhere around inside me. After two days or so my parents were finally back together again. My family was complete, and I wanted it to stay that way forever.

The third thing that I want you to know is after my parents got back together again, my life changed forever. I just found out last year that my mom was pregnant with my little brother. He has been the best thing that happened to me so far because it was an amazing thing to have a little baby brother. I recalled times when I begged my mom for another brother since it was three girls and a younger brother. I wanted a baby brother and now it's finally happening. My baby brother was finally born on April 11th around 7am. He was very healthy, letting out the loudest cries I ever heard from a baby. Right now, he is 1 year and 5 months old, a baby that rather walks around naked and likes to argue. If he didn't come along I'm sure I will be stuck in the same old boring life, but with my baby around, there is just so many things to do that I'm busy all the time. I'm really happy and glad that he came along. Even though Junior causes a lot of trouble around the house and does the most impossible things for a 1 year old, there is one thing that I always remind myself of—he came and made my life brighter.

With you reading this I hope you would understand what I have gone through. Sometimes during a school day when I'm feeling down in class, I don't like to show it, nor do I want to be bothered; I hope you would understand that. I'm glad that I was able to share this with you and share the things that I have kept deep inside me. I'm also glad to be sharing my bright times with you through this letter as well.

Sincerely,
Thank God She Could Speak English

ALL SORTS OF FEELINGS

Dear Teacher,
I wish my teacher knew that it's a little rough right now. My grandpa is not feeling too well. About a week or so we were all at his house. We ate

and had a good time. But later that week, my dad and my uncles dressed grandpa in his Hmong clothes. This means his life is nearing the end. He couldn't move. We all thought he was going go into eternal rest. That night was one of the scariest nights I have had. It was the first time I have ever seen my grandma cry. It hurts watching her cry. I was crying too. We were all crying. My aunts, cousins, uncles and people I didn't even know. My cousins went first to say their "thank yous" to him. We were in his room for a good hour or so. It was my turn next. I said, "Thank you for teaching me stuff I have never learned about in life." I was bawling my eyes out. My grandma kept on telling me to not cry, no more after this. She kept on saying that it's going to be okay. She told me not to worry. I have never seen my whole family in this much pain before, especially my grandma. I just never want it to happen again. Right now, he is in a better condition. We just hope that he gets better.

I honestly don't know what to do. A little of everything: a little sadness, a little confusion, and a little scared, that is how I feel. What I want you to know is what can I do to help the family. Helping out is one of the things my family taught me and yet I can't do anything. I'm more scared than all of those things earlier but like how I was taught, I just have to face it and do it. Man-up. Don't be a wuss. Not everyone is going hold your hand forever. I say all those things in class to other people because I don't want them to become like me. I am scared to talk in front of the class or scared of starting a conversation. It's a frightening just thinking about it right now; life for sure, is a journey. They say it's not the destination, but the journey. I agree and disagree. It's both. The journey represents trial and error. Thank you for listening.

Sincerely,
All Sorts of Feelings

THE NAVY DAUGHTER

Dear Teacher,

This my story that I'm going to share with you. I came from a family that has a lot of support and we were okay with money. When my mom and dad had me, my dad was only there to see a little bit of me at the hospital. Then he had to go to the Navy, so most of my childhood I stayed with my mom and she would take me everywhere and change my diaper and just make sure I was healthy. I was born in Georgia where my paternal grandparents and my family lived for a long time. When my dad came back from the Navy I remember traveling a lot. When I came back from the trip, my uncles would babysit me.

The second thing I'm going to share with you is my childhood. When I was 7, I lived in Menomonie, a small town where only white kids lived. When we moved inside our house that summer, I had no friends and we had a few family members living there. I remember going to school on September 5 and having all the white people look at me and just stared. I was nervous, but my teacher came up to me and said, "Hi what is your name?" I replied back, "I… am… Am…an…. da." My teacher said, "Wow, what a beautiful name." I thanked her and smiled back at her while she walked back up to the front of the room. I wished my teacher would have known that I was alone, really shy, and I wanted to make new friends.

Another thing I wished my teacher knew was while growing up as a teenager I was treated differently. I felt that I was treated wrong because everyone hated me. When I was living in Elk Mound, I hated it. Honestly, I wished that I was somewhere else because I never saw my parents much. I always got yelled at for little things and asked to do everything because in the Hmong culture women are supposed to take care of the household. My mom always told me that I had to do the dishes and cook, and it was to prepare me for my marriage and the future. I thought she was lying to me, so I never really took the advice. I was always worried about having fun because I was still a kid. I always wanted to have a sleepover, but my mom and dad never let me. My parents always depended on me to do things. I love my parents, but sometimes I feel as if they're punishing me too much and making me do everything. I was always confused about that and I never really understood it. Sometimes I would get so mad I would run to my room and close my door really hard and lock the door.

Lastly my life right now is good as I'm learning right now how to better manage time and go to school and work. I love my parents and I'm in that stage where I am learning to say, "Yes, I will do that for you" because my parents need my help. My dad is working 2 jobs just to go to Laos with my mom for their anniversary. I can tell that he is so tired and works everyday even on the weekends to provide for my family too. That is all that I would like you to know about me. I'm doing good and life for me is hard right now, but I will get over it.

Sincerely,
The Navy Daughter

Wish I was Closer to My Teacher

Dear Teacher,
I wish you would know that I hesitate a lot to answer questions even

when I know that it's the right answer. I don't really understand why I do that. I'm also very afraid to ask questions even though it's your job to help me with whatever.

A few years ago, a very dreadful event happened, my dad passed away tragically. I was 10 or 11 at the time, so growing up was very difficult. My dad's side of the family doesn't "love" us anymore because of multiple reasons, such as my mom never going over to help anymore.

I mean I'm always happy unless something is really bothering me. Anyways growing up, I never realized how much my mother suffered just to provide and take care of us and make sure we had everything we wanted. My mom had gotten remarried to a relative on my dad's side of the family, and he is from Laos. After they had gotten married, I slowly realized that my mom stopped caring because my step-dad doesn't love us. Don't get me wrong, for I know she loves us a lot, but I just didn't feel it anymore. The first few years I was the only one who realized that he didn't love us, nor love my mom. One reason why I know he didn't love any of us because he wouldn't let my mom spend money on us, but always made her send money to his family. But I know she loves us emotionally and physically. During the time my mom had stopped showing us love, I just remembered it being the saddest ever I have been because I grew up with no parents. I had no one to remind me about my homework or brush my teeth or tell me that they are proud of me. It was always, "Why are you not like your cousin? She's skinny, smart, and beautiful." Maybe because she always had support? My mom loves us a lot now. She changed so much, and I feel so loved now. Maybe because I don't live with her anymore?

I also wish that the teachers would have closer relationships with their students. I feel like if a teacher were to have a bond with their students, there would be a higher rate of kids who graduate.In my family I have 4 siblings; I'm the 5th child and the youngest. Out of the 4 oldest, only one graduated high school. I really want to make my family proud and prove to our dad's side of the family that we're not just a few kids with no dad and no education. Also, my dad's side of the family don't "love" us anymore because my mom got remarried to a younger person.

I also really wished the teachers would care about our feelings more. Some kids go through so much and just need to know that they have someone to talk to. Also, I would love if some teachers notice kids who get bullied and help. I know that suicide cases are caused by bullies!! I just want everyone to feel safe and comfortable.

Sincerely,
Wish I was Closer to My Teacher

4333

Dear Teacher,

I'm that goofy kid in your class, and this is a letter so that you get to know your only and only Goofy Kid. I'm never really a down person because I'm usually always a very happy and energetic individual, but when I'm down I'm usually just unusually quiet. So, if one day I'm just really quiet, I'm probably just having a bad day, or I didn't get enough sleep. For Hmong class, I really need help on all of the sections (reading, writing, speaking, etc...), so I'm probably going to take some more time than others to learn the lessons.

It's funny because when I was a toddler I was actually really fluent in Hmoob, but once I started Kindergarten I started speaking English for the first time and since English was more important to communicate to others at the time (most of the teachers and kids at my school were *mekas* [Caucasian] and *khejdub* [Blacks]), I just focused on it more and lost my Hmong in the process. Also, I'm in sports, so I would really appreciate it if you gave me some slack because I get home everyday at 8pm; therefore, I don't have a lot of time for all my homework, projects, essays, etc.

I was born in a small town in the California. I lived there for about 1 ½ years then I moved out here to Minnesota. I went back to visit California in 2016 because my grandpa had died of a car accident there. So, then we drove all the way over there, which was about a 24-hour drive. But I'm happy I went because I got to explore the town I was born in, and also meet lots of family that I have never seen in my life. It was intimidating at first because there were so many people who were like, "Wow, I remembered holding you in my arms when you were a baby!" and "You are so handsome", and "You look just like your mom." But in my mind, I was like, "I don't even know you all," but then once I got more comfortable with them, we started becoming closer as family.

My dad has kidney failure, and he is currently on dialysis. He actually started experiencing kidney problems before my paternal grandpa's death. He used to always work out everyday, run, and eat healthy, but suddenly he started to throw up randomly, getting sick often and losing his appetite. As a result, he also started coming home early from work often too because of how sick he was. Then my mom started to worry and took him to the hospital at night, and they diagnosed him with kidney failure. Ever since that day he's been on treatment with dialysis. If you didn't know what dialysis is, it's basically a machine the size of 2 printers, and what it does is it takes out extra fluids out from your blood (water, toxins, etc...). It's used by patients whose kidneys don't function properly enough to filter out these fluids. My dad has to perform dialysis about 3-4 times a week. He would have to go a medical professional at the hospital to have this performed, but since my mom is a medical professional, he can do it from the comfort of home instead of going to a hospital every single time he needs it. But I feel like my father has changed now that he's having problems with his kidneys. Because when he first started doing dialysis he wasn't sold by the idea because it involves needles, but then the doctor said, "You probably will live at the most, 3 months, if you don't take dialysis." So, he usually gets mad easier now, and forces us to stay in the living room. But then my mom tells me that he only does this because he thinks he has limited time with the kids and wants to spend all the time he can with us.

So again, I'm the one goofy, funny, quirky kid in class that is always talking. And by this letter to you, I hope you got to know me better as not just a student, but as a person and human being also.

Sincerely,
4333

ALMOST PRINCESS OF THAILAND

Dear Teacher,

I'm new to this area and this school. Here I don't know many people, so I don't have many people to talk to or hangout with. I must say I really do miss my old school and my old friends, but I know that there are greater things here for me and I can learn in the ways I didn't before. I'm glad that you are someone I can relate and talk to, even though we just met not too long ago.

I have many things I would like to talk about, but I don't know what kinds of things I should say to keep everything interesting. I'm a pretty quiet person, so I don't speak about myself a lot to others, I just tend to listen, but here I am. There are three things I thought about that I want people to learn from my experiences and understand my hardships, but also enjoy an interesting story of mine. So here I go.

First, I found out that my father was supposed to be the king of Thailand. How? It was a long time before I was born, my parents and siblings went to an aunt's house and they got to meet this Hmong story teller. She had gray and brown eyes and she was so careful with everything she did. Supposedly this woman was very smart, and she knew a lot. She was like a shaman, but even more powerful. My father asked if she could tell him something about him and she did so. She took his hand and read it; she was so amazing. She then told my father and my mother that when my father was going to be reborn, he carried the letter to become the Thai king, but on the way, he felt thirsty and he stopped by a woman and asked her for some water. During that time, he must have dropped the paper. The current Thai King now, probably picked up the piece of paper my father dropped. Then something weird happened and he magically went into the stomach of the lady who he asked for some water from. That is why my father had 7 daughters. He must have taken his life with him, but not the person's paper. And that is how he became my grandma's son. Today, I still wonder why my father just didn't keep on going, but I'm glad he got me a good grandma.

Secondly, my parents have been divorced for 6 years now and I live with my mother. I do get to see my father here and there. Both my parents are remarried as well, both their new significant others are from overseas. I'm not disappointed, but I just wished they didn't divorce. Fortunately, I know that they are happier now and I'm happy for them. My father has 2 kids with his wife. I love my cute half-siblings so much. By the way, I don't get to see my childhood cousins anymore, so that saddens me a lot. I do get to see everyone once in awhile, so that is good.

Living with my mother is harder for me now because in the future I'm not able to marry not only my dad's clan, but also my step-father's clan as well. I disagree with her just because her husband is not my biological father, so she should not have put me and my other sisters under his family clan name. I still don't accept my step-parents, but I respect them. I don't communicate with them often though, but I have learned some Hmong lessons from them. Thanks to them I'm able to ask someone who is fluent in Hmong to help me.

Lastly, I went through my first mental break down in 6th grade. It was so sad, I remember crying about the things that I had been going through. I had so much drama in my life and my siblings would tell me I'm stupid or that I wouldn't get anywhere in life. I held everything that happened in till I broke and bursted into tears. I was alone at this time, and I just couldn't tell anyone. Just because everyone was so quick to judge and say this or that to break me. I didn't appreciate people saying this kind of nonsense about me to me. I felt like if people wanted to be honest with me then maybe they could have just kept it to themselves because it hurts me. It deeply put a hole in my heart and soul. I figured I like it when people are honest because I can always prove them wrong or I can thank them for their act of honesty. After this break down, it taught me many things. It taught me that people will put you down, you will cry once in a while. You have to go through some obstacles to get to where you want to be, so no matter the kind of obstacles you go through, you will make it out and show your worth. I still think about those things. Now I don't cry about it anymore because I have bigger things I can put my mind to and I look forward to success.

Today I'm pursuing my dreams and I will move forward even if I don't get the career I want. I'm still a bit confused on my future career, but it's becoming clearer what I'm doing with my life and what I want to do. Many bad things happened to me at school and fear was one. Now that I'm in high school, I thought maybe I will get over it and just be independent. Sadly, fear holds on and will keep doing so until I give out. Going to such a big school and being new here, it's difficult to get around, especially because of the schedules. I like to think that I can do many things because I'm so independent. I have grown up well and I'm not independent because I didn't have my parents or siblings by my side. They were there, but I just grew to be independent because I just worked better, and I could do things my way. I'm open-minded when it comes to collaborating, but when I'm alone I work so much better even though I might not comprehend everything. My independence was built because I know someday I'm going places because someday no one is going to keep helping me. Someday my sisters and brothers will ask for help and I will do so to help. I know someday my parents are going to be in a better place and I will not have a shoulder to cry on, or to have someone to tell me I'm doing something wrong or give me a hand. I know I will make my life very successful and I will be going somewhere I don't even plan to be. I don't know what the future holds for me, but I'm excited to see. I'm excited to see what kind of new things I will try, what kind of obstacles I will be facing, and how others will react. I'm proud of what I'm doing, and I will continue to do it and make myself better each day. And here is where it ends, this might no have been only about me, but this is what I wanted you to know about me.

Overall, I'm thankful for all the opportunities that I get. I will be taking advantage of them because I don't get many of these opportunities. Being a little selfish doesn't hurt. Thanks for your time and effort to be reading this far, but I know I might have written too much; I had a lot to say. I had much more to say, but I will end it here. I would be relieved if this was to interesting you too.

Sincerely,
Almost Princess of Thailand

THINGS UNKNOWN

Dear Teacher,
I wish you knew that I have only three memories of my biological father. I wish my teachers knew that my mother had to play both roles for four years, until she met my step-father. I wish you knew that not having my biological father around is still a sensitive subject for me.

I wish you knew that I grew up lonely. I was the girl who didn't realize that I didn't inherit the communication and social skills that other people my age inherited. I wish you didn't make me the odd one out because of it. I never was one to have more than two friends at once. I have always been the mysterious, quiet girl. My mother constantly heard that her Hmong daughter was very capable of success, but her daughter was just too shy to take advantage of it. For years, my mother has encouraged me to raise my hand more to speak up. It wasn't easy then and it's not any easier now. I wish you knew that, everyday, I'm trying to overcome this.

I wish you knew that on days where I can gather the courage to tell them that I'm having a bad day; it means my day is going extremely bad because I don't let little things get to me. I wish you knew that, at times, my anxiety takes over and it's hard for me to focus in class. Outside of school, I don't have much time to myself. Most of the time, I will stay up late or start my days early to do my school work, and sometimes, I will not finish. It results in me coming to school half asleep because of the lack of sleep. I wish you wouldn't criticize my time management skills. I wish you wouldn't misunderstand when I'm half asleep in class. I wish you knew that I'm trying my best

Sincerely,
Things Unknown

卝 卝 卝 卝 卝 卝 卝 卝 卝 卝 卝 卝 卝 卝 卝

I Wish I Would of Have Someone to Talk to

Dear Teacher,
When I was a little girl, my parents were always fighting. I don't know if it's okay to share something so personal, especially because it's not entirely my story, but my perspective. However, I do know that it's something that has stuck with me since the age that I was old enough to comprehend that my parents were not together anymore, and they would never be together again. It has always been difficult to open up to people about this dark side of my life and I could say that only very few people actually know the details between what happened and how I personally feel about it. I guess that is why I'm comfortable with sharing part of my life with you as my teacher. Because you are a Hmong woman, a wife, a mother,

you would probably understand how I feel.

My mom and dad got married at an extremely young age and because of that my mom never wanted me to get into relationships at a young age. My mom eloped to marry my dad at a young age. I think my mom and dad were happy together. At least that is what I heard. Then I hear other stories from my family about how my dad had always been abusive and mean to my mom. However, to me it didn't seem like it or my mom didn't make it seem that way. I guess only my mom and dad know the actual story to all that has happened. However, I'm too scared to ask for details just because it's such a dark past in my mom's life. I'm sure she has recovered from it, but I would hate to bring it up because I know it has scarred her.

Growing up, I have always been a little angry with my dad, but the love is still there. I grew up without him, yet I love him, and I'm not sure why. How can you love someone that you spent most of your life without and you have very few memories of? Until this day, I still have flashbacks of being with my dad and I was actually a daddy's girl as a kid, because of course every kid sees their mom as "mean." Besides that, my memory of my dad as a little girl is blurred.

I do remember one thing clearly though and sometimes I wish I didn't remember it because it's such a painful memory. I believe when we still lived in Colorado, my mom and us lived with my dad's brother and his kids along with my auntie. I don't remember if it was after they had moved out and we remained in their house or if they just were not home. However, one night we were all home alone and I was with my older brother in the living room. At the time, my younger brother was still a baby only, maybe only a couple months old. That night, I witnessed my dad physically abusing my mom. I saw the way he grabbed her and threw her around like she wasn't anything. I saw the way he choked her and slammed her against the wall… it has become something I can never forget. I remember my mom took my brother and I to the other room and I could hear them fighting. I started to cry. I didn't know what was going on, but I knew something wasn't right. Knowing that my mom went through all of that alone makes me feel guilty even though I know I wasn't at fault. I just wish I was able to comfort her at the time and I wish I had respected her growing up the way I do now because she deserves the world.

In the past few years living in Minnesota, my dad has become sick. He is currently diagnosed with a medical condition. Being a traditional Hmong shaman family, my dad's side is broke. Thankfully though, my auntie has the biggest heart in the world and has set foot into helping my dad with his medication and getting better. That is all I wish for. My dad has changed in so many ways and I'm glad that he has decided to turn his life around even if it seems too late and he can never fully recover. That is all that really matters. I love my dad. However, I do blame him for the decisions he made years ago, but I forgive him because what can I do? I can't spend the rest of my life being angry at him, especially when he is trying to make a change. Growing up without a dad has always been hard for me, especially on Father's Day. I have always envied girls who have their father in their life because I wish I did too.

I wished I would have had someone I could talk to when I had boyfriend problems because my mother can be a little crazy (sarcasm). I wished I would have had someone I could talk to when I couldn't talk to my mom. A father figure is nothing compared to your actual father. I'm in contact with my dad now and I couldn't be happier. Every now and then my brother and I try to send money to my dad due to the fact that he can't afford to work. He is living in a boarding home and they don't do the best at taking care of him, but it works. Whatever happens though, I know my brother and I will be there. I don't think that this is the most stressful thing that is on my mind though.

I guess I'm stressing about something that is taking place in the future, but it could also be something that can happen at anytime. Besides that fact, I'm trying to work hard. Going to school and working 4-10 p.m after school is not easy to balance. Hard work pays off though and I'm aiming to live the life that my grandparents, my mom and my dad couldn't live. I know that is what they want for not just me, but my brothers as well. I go to school looking happy and full of joy almost everyday. It's almost a shock to my friends when I'm sad. However, this is one big part of my life that I struggle on my own trying to fight everyday when I'm alone. I always wonder about the "What ifs" and I have been told that there are none and that I should not think about it because it is what it is. So, it's not my family or my mom that I'm fighting with. It's a battle that I'm constantly fighting alone with myself and I just can not seem to let go. Who knows? Maybe I will never be able to let go of it. Maybe I will heal from it and maybe learn from it.

A few years ago, my mom took us kids and we fled here to Minnesota to live with my mom's side of the family. They are Christians, so growing up in a Christian household, I have learned to forgive. Coming to MN may have been the best thing that has happened to my mom and us kids. She was able to start new and so were we. It has been an awesome 12 years living in MN, but I still miss my home, Colorado. It's funny that whenever I go to Colorado, it does feel like home. I'm not sure how to explain this sensation, but for some reason, it just feels like I belong there. And who knows? Maybe I will move back someday. However, for now, I'm aiming to become the best that I can for my family.

Besides this battle that I'm fighting alone, I can say that I don't feel like the luckiest Hmong girl. I have been so blessed to have an awesome family and the most loving mother in this world. Not every Hmong girl feels the same way I do, but I can honestly say that I would never trade my mom for anyone. So, now I just want to take the time to say

"Thank You" my teacher for allowing us students to do this assignment. To be able to share a story that we find difficulty expressing. It honestly makes a big difference knowing that someone actually cares to know our individual stories that we can't express to just anyone. I would also like to thank you for being able to share your story with us as your students. It's never easy sharing a story that you were never able to easily express. So, thank you again for taking the time to read part of my life!

Sincerely,
I Wish I Would of Have Someone to Talk to

TRYING SO HARD

Dear Teacher,
This has been a stressful 4 years of high school. I'm glad I could spend my 4 years of high school with you, someone who has helped me with my education, someone who taught me the meaning of education and just everything that every Asian girl would need to know as life goes.

I have been that loud girl in your class with good grade, but shy in her other classes. I'm that someone who would always ask you, "Is this right? Or am I wrong?" As a little Hmong girl growing up, I see the struggle of my parents working many hours just to get my siblings and I what we wanted. I try hard in school, so I could go far in life and make my parents proud. I know and understand that everyone around the world has their own struggles in life, and I know you do as well. I wish you knew these three things about me.

First and foremost, in every Hmong household, parents want a good *nyab* that would help them whenever they need, but my sister-in-law is not like what we expect. When I first saw my my sister-in-law, she looked gentle and looked like she could be a good *nyab* to my parents. After three days of the Hmong tradition, where a new daughter-in-law rests, she got lazy and stayed in her room everyday. Everytime when my siblings and I come home, we wouldn't see her. She is not a good *nyab* like how my siblings and my parents thought she would be during the first days that she came to live with us. Now, she would talk smack about my family and blast us all up on Facebook even when we didn't do anything to her. It makes my parents disappointed and it makes them sad. As for me, I'm a very sensitive person and it's hard to see my parents being sad and disappointed for this reason. My parents are great parents and they don't deserve someone who treats them so cruel. Whenever it comes to family gatherings, she is being the nice *nyab* that she could, but deep down my relatives don't know how she treats us at home. Everytime when she brought food like fruits and snacks, she wouldn't share it with us, but called for her relative to come eat them. It's just so disappointing to see that my brother sees everything, but he is not doing anything to help it.

Secondly, I wished you knew what I was going through outside of school. Being a Hmong girl, my parents expect so much more from me than from my brothers. Being a son, you get as much freedom as you want, while the girls can't have much freedom. We could barely get out of the house. My brothers went out late at night with no phone calls from my parents chasing after them. While being a Hmong girl, my parents called me every five minutes telling me to come home even when I just left the house for less than one hour. I struggle every time telling my parents to treat us the same as the boys. Just because we're are different from them doesn't mean we should be treated differently. My family makes me feel like I can't breathe or have freedom like my brothers does.

Lastly, I wished you and my parents know that I have to try as hard as I can to do well like other kids. Being a Hmong teenager, my parent only motivatie me with their words to inspire me to try harder in school everyday. But harsh words and uninspiring words is what makes me fall each day. When I started high school four years ago, my parents started to compare my siblings and I with my cousins saying this and that. And little do they know, those words and comparisons are bringing us down to the floor. Each day I feel weak, and don't feel like trying anymore in school. Even though every trimester, I change from A to B honor rolls, I wanted you and my parents to know that I have tried, tried with every strength I have and with every knowledge I have learned throughout my 13 years of schooling.

Being in your class everyday, writing daily prompt journals every morning gives me tears and I wish you would have read every journal of mine; I wished you would have read deep down and tell me it would be alright, and that everything was just a bad dream and it wouldn't happen ever again. I hope that you will be the one who I can tell my everyday stories to and who could listen to me and not cut me off every time I begin to talk.

Sincerely,
Trying So Hard

YOUNG MOM

Dear Teacher,

I will be writing about things that I would love you to read about. I'm an open person and I normally don't mind sharing my story.

The first thing to know about me is that I dropped-out of school last year because I was going through lots of family issues and personal issues. To start, I had gotten a divorce a week before school started. I left home because I couldn't stand how my family was at the time. I moved in with my co-worker and eventually he and I became a couple.

Then I wasn't able to bus to my new school, so I made the choice to drop-out, and to take online class or alternative school. Then soon after I found out I was pregnant. Once I found out and told my boyfriend, we were overjoyed to know we would become parents, but then reality hit us faster than we would have thought. What we were bringing in wasn't enough for us to live on and we needed more, so my boyfriend went to get a higher paying job. We decided to find better jobs and it backfired. Both he and I became jobless and then we found out that I was having a high-risk pregnancy. My baby was much smaller than the average baby. Due to that, we saw the doctors two times a week. Six months in my pregnancy I got a job and I was reconnecting with my family again. Like every other parent, they were not happy about their young daughter being pregnant, but they forgave us.

They offered us to come live with them after my one month post partum. When we moved in, I was working two jobs and raise my son. I had a conversation with my parents and they encouraged me to go back to school because I only had one year left. I applied to go back to school for my son and that is why I'm here in your class.

Secondly, I just hope to have understood you, my teachers. I hope that teachers would encourage me to keep going and check up on me. I have had a hard time at home with my son and homework; my boyfriend has just started his new job, so it's pretty hard too now. I'm trying my best and I hope you as a teacher will lead me to a successful way to life and graduate. I'm looking forward for this year with you, my teacher.

Sincerely,
Young Mom

ALMOST SAW DEATH IN ARMS

Dear Teacher,
I wish you knew that a lot has changed in my life and I'm not the same person I once was. When I was a child, I didn't care about the world, nor did I care about what was going on. I was a very happy girl that had no troubles in life. I would always look at the bright side of things and tell myself that everything was okay, but I was very lonely. I didn't have anyone other than my family.

I remember that I hated going to school because I wanted to stay home with my mother more than anything. Sometimes I would even cry when she left for work. I missed her dearly whenever I was at school or she was at work. As of now, I still do miss her because I only see her for about 15 minutes in the morning then I don't get to see her until late that night. Despite this, she does call me from time to time to check on how I am doing, so I'm glad to at least hear her voice even though I can't see her. I love my mother very much, but that doesn't mean I don't love my father.

I love them both equally. Even though I feel like they don't understand me sometimes, I know that deep down, they still support me no matter what.

I hate telling this story, but I've got to be real. Here we go. I can't remember when it happened, but I was quite young. My father was caught cheating behind my mother and she almost died in front of me in the bathroom that she had hidden in. Can you imagine someone who is still young losing their mother right in front of them? I was so confused and so lost, I didn't know what was going on! I cried and screamed, so that she didn't leave me! Luckily, she came back to us and we lived life as if nothing had ever happened. I'm so grateful that we're all still here as a big family. Despite having our ups and downs, it's just how we show our love to each other.

I was always alone during elementary, and I never had any friends to be or play with. I was the lonely, shy, perfectionist who would always follow the rules and try my best. Sure, I did have friends, but I lost them as time flew by. It wasn't until upper elementary grade school when I truly made a friend. I thought we would always be together throughout our school life, but it wasn't until 9th grade that everything changed. She abandoned me for her other friends. She had forgotten who I was. I feel like everyone I knew from before is now distancing themselves away from me. I'm dead to everyone. I'm invisible to everyone unless I make the first move, but it's fine. I endured this pain for a while now. Even if I do lose all of my friends, at least I still have myself to look after. No matter how much it hurts, I will just have to carry on like a broken bird who lost its wings.

My life is not so easy as it looks on the outside. I'm a girl who feels so much pressure when it comes to expectations, especially from my parents. I tell myself I must do my best or else I will never be able to face my family properly. That is why I push myself so hard to the point that I'm not even thinking about things reasonably. It's as if I'm giving people what they want instead of doing what I want. Am I impressing people because I want to...? Or am I just impressing them to prove that I'm actually useful? My dad usually tells me this, "You go to school, but you don't learn anything?" What does he take me for? I try so hard to push myself in all of my classes, so I get an 'A'. I try so hard to get onto that "A" honor roll to get a certificate. I try so hard to make them proud of me, but with him saying that, it just lowers my esteem. Well, it's not like my esteem wasn't already low enough. I just hope my efforts didn't go to waste and I didn't suffer for nothing.

Over the past few years, I have been having a lot of anxiety because I was born as a very shy girl. I hate talking, and I don't like meeting people either. I can't seem to get myself out of this crippling shell. I feel like if I express myself, I will get looked down upon and be judged by those around me. That is why I shut myself away from this world. I didn't want to face any more pain or suffering. The anxiety lives on within me, but I know eventually, I will have to open my broken shell. I'm slowly getting used to speaking, but I don't know. I'm not quite there yet, but at least I'm trying to open myself up more.

I don't know how many times I broke down and wanted to tear up. I sometimes spill these tears of mine for no reason. There are days when I feel emotionally sad and there are days when I don't even know how to feel. I'm not happy, but I'm not sad either. These emotions of sadness and happiness, I don't understand them at all. I do understand one thing, it makes up who I am, and it proves that I'm a human being, just like everyone else. Never had I once wanted to give up living. If I did, I would be leaving all of those I dearly loved behind. I don't ever want to give them so much pain to endure, all because of me. That is why I'm going to live my life to the fullest with those I love. I will never lose myself as long as I see the open path that guides me safely to where I want to be.

As of now, I like to think I'm in a much happier place, but I don't know. I've still got a lot to learn about myself and this world. I'm not alone though. I made a few new friends and I've got many people that are supporting me. No matter how cruel, no matter how hard, no matter how painful it is. I will continue to live life with no regrets! This was just the beginning of the battle, now comes the real one.

To you who is reading this letter, know you are not alone. No matter how dark and gloomy this world may be, there is still a bit of color out there that shines in us all. Even you. Treasure those that matter to you and never lose sight of them. Dry those tears away and smile like you never had before. Never stop believing and never lose yourself. Even if we go our separate ways, we'll never be apart. I was very happy to have be given such an opportunity to meet a person like you. Thank you for everything. I will never forget your kindness and just how special of a person you were to me.

Sincerely,
Almost Saw Death in Arm

LOST IN THE MIX

Dear Teacher,
I greatly appreciate that I can share this about myself. During school hours I used to be a very quiet kid, an introvert. I still am now, but I'm learning to engage and get out of my comfort zone. I'm not typically the

straight A student who knows all the answers, although I wish I was. I believe I'm smart, but I just tend to work at a slower pace compared to my peers. I beat myself up at the fact that I don't understand situations at times.

For my entire life, I have lived in Wisconsin. There were not many Hmong people where I lived besides my family. I always went to a predominantly Black and White school. Being the only Asian or even Hmong person was tough because where did I fit in? So, growing up, I only spoke English. I barely have any knowledge of the Hmong culture or speaking the language. I don't blame anyone for it, but myself. I never sought out anyone for help. I feel like a disgrace for not knowing anything. I hope this class will open my eyes with a new perspective on how I view things and educate me with my own culture.

My parents were young when they had my siblings and me. I'm the youngest of my two siblings. Growing up wasn't sunshine and rainbows, although I sometimes wish it was because life would be so much different compared to what it's now. My parents' divorce impacted my life greatly. My parents divorced when I was very young, but it was the fighting for custody that often made me gloomy. It lasted for many years. During the whole custody battle, at the time, I lived with my dad, wanting to live with my mom. My step-mom wasn't the greatest person. I was after all, just her step-child.

As you may know, I moved from Wisconsin towards the end of summer. It was the hardest decision I could have ever make for myself. I lived with mom before moving. To keep it short, we didn't have the best relationship. She was a negative impact in my life. A so called "figure" in my life who didn't believe in me, who would joke I wouldn't make it to college because I'm not the best at things and I have no dreams. I made the decision to move because I didn't feel loved and welcomed in my own home by my own parent.

Thank you so much for listening and feeling my pain.

Sincerely,
Lost in the Mix

THOUGHTFUL FRIEND

Dear Teacher,

I have learned so much in Hmong class, within the first mid-trimester. I have learned the tones, how to sound out hmong words, and even back-stories about our Hmong words.

My Hmong classmates know a lot about our teacher or at least we know him more than he knows us. So, what I want to do is to tell him and other people some things that I'm comfortable sharing. There are times in life where everyone goes through, and lessons everyone learns while living, and I want to personally share what I experienced because sometimes it's important to express and let things off my chest.

Let us start off small and work into building up to the deeper stuff. I will not be getting way into detail with everything, but I will just say the basics. I have lost so many important people in my life such as two important people in my life that I was somewhat close with. One of them was my baby cousin. She had a heart defect and passed away on Christmas.

A few years ago, my *yawm txiv* passed away from cancer. This affected me and my family a lot and it taught me so many things. During the funerals I saw so many of my relatives, whether they are from here or out of state. I had no choice but to help with the funeral for my yawm txiv and I'm glad I helped. I was there 24/7 and saw every person walk in and out through the funeral doors. They all had cried at least once because they all had a great bond with him; some of them didn't even have a close relationship with *yawm txiv,* but they still cried. Looking at those people I have learned that family is important, or friends are important. I have known that, but I just noticed it more than I used to. I personally went through a suicidal stage before my *yawm txiv's* funeral, and it was to the point where it was getting out of control. I had a few family and friends that helped me stop and become a better version of myself. They all told me the same thing over and over and over again, but I just didn't listen until my *yawm txiv* and baby cousin passed away. It hit me so hard in the brain that I just stopped being suicidal and thought, "Why am I so stupid for doing all of this?"

Everyday 24/7 I think about my life and ask myself if I'm doing well. Sometimes, I have my bad days, and sometimes I have my good days. These past few days/weeks/months, I have been having bad days because right now I'm just going through a lot, but that's besides the point. Recently I thought about my group of friends, and others, I thought about the people I surround myself with. I thought about how they act around me, compared to others, or sometimes I observe their moods. I'm an observant person when I want to be. I choose my friends by how they treat others and how they act around people, and their personalities. My friends say I'm popular around the Asian community. I guess I know a lot of asians, and a lot of asians know me, but I don't think I'm popular.

Popular is a big word. I have learned to choose friends wisely, just because they say, "I will be here if you need me" or "I will always have your back," when reality hits and something really does happen, they are not going to be there. They are not going be true to the words they said.

I think about it, and they could be just saying it, just to say it, or they are just trying to find out what you're thinking about or what you are going through. They could be using you. I feel like they are not really going to be there for you. The only people who are going to be there for you is your family, especially your parents. Don't trust every single one of your friends, as they could be back stabbing you, or doing all these things you don't even know.

I'm a very open person, and I can be shy sometimes. For the most part, I'm very open. I tend to talk a lot. I don't know if that is a good thing or a bad thing, but I love to talk to people and meet new people. Back in my middle school years, I was such a horrible person. I would bully people. I was well-known at my middle, so everyone wanted to have beef with me, and they got the beef they wanted. I had so much drama in middle school, but when I hit ninth-grade, over the summer I met my ex, and he changed me into a better person.

He taught me how to be loving and caring, and he showed me how to control my anger. He also taught me to be open and talk to a lot of people. He taught me so many things, if it were not for him, I wouldn't be where I am today. He had a big impact in my life, and I'm glad he was in it.

The point is, there is going to be that one person who makes you realize some things that you don't even realize and change you into a better person. There is always going to be that one person that is going to be your role model that you look up to and follow. For me, my ex was that person. It's weird to say, but it's the truth. Overall, you learn a lot going through life, whether it's lectures or lessons you learn while going through some things. Sometimes you might not learn the simplest things in life until years pass by. Some people learn quick, some people learn fast, it depends on who you are.

I just know that life is hard, and it's supposed to be challenging.

It's never meant to be easy, in the first place. Choose the right path you think best fits you, and it doesn't matter if it's good or bad. It's what YOU believe fits you. Don't depend on other people's opinions. Not everything in life is going to be the way you want it, but if you really believe and try, then maybe some of your dreams can become reality and true. You are alive for a reason, so make it worth a living. Make it crazy. Live it to the fullest. Live it like if it was your last. You truly deserve it.

Sincerely,
Thoughtful Friend

Feels Like the Only Child

Dear Teacher,
I'm a person who is a very antisocial introvert. When it comes to meeting people online, they seem fun or cool, and I can introduce myself and try to be friends with them. When I'm with my friends, I feel at ease and can easily be myself when around them and have fun and laugh.

On the other hand, I'm a shy person in general, and when I'm in a room full of people I don't know, I usually don't talk much. Out in public, I could care less about how people view me, so I act myself and have fun with my day. But in classrooms there are my classmates who I would like to be friends with, I just don't usually know how to advance my conversations with them. I don't tend to speak in groups or even with a partner I don't know about, so the conversation usually ends up a bit awkward.

Last summer my dad and mom got divorced. My mom moved to Colorado, and my little brother and I stayed with my dad. A few months ago, my older half-brother left to go live with his girlfriend, so the house is more empty than usual. My dad works first shift, my little brother goes to school, and my grandma is off somewhere in the morning until around 3. So, it's been like this for about a year, and now my cousin lives with us and helps pay the rent.

Often when I get stressed and bored I tend to play games with my friends to relieve that stress and have fun, but my dad and grandma think otherwise. My grandma is a person who is very negative and tends to drag you down. My dad is also stressed about work, my grandma, and fixing the house. Since my little brother is too young and my grandma is too old, I have to help my dad.

I'm not an only child, but I feel like one, I have an older half-brother, older half-sister, and a younger brother. I wish I had siblings the same age as me. Sometimes I even feel like wanting a twin brother or sister. My dad says that family is more important than friends because friends will come and go, which I can agree that family is important, but friends are just as important also. I sometimes spend time with family and have fun, but when I got my phone last year, I started to hangout with friends outside school. I had tons of fun like going ice skating and Karaoke-ing with friends.

I keep most of my feelings and other things on the inside and don't share them much. People don't talk to me much, so I don't usually talk. If they ask me what is wrong I tend to say nothing because either I'm not in the mood, I don't care, or I don't know how to put it into words. I admit, I'm lazy most of the time and most things I don't tend to do, but other times I can be a hard worker and try my hardest. I don't say much, so not many people know a lot about me. I'm a weird person and want to be friendly, but don't know how to approach them most of the time. I wish I could have been more of a extrovert or an ambivert, but I'm not. This is who I am. Thanks for reading my story.

Sincerely,
Feels Like the Only Child

❦+❦+❦+❦+❦+❦+❦+❦+❦+❦+❦+❦+❦+❦

FUTURE PSYCHOLOGIST

Dear Teacher,

I wish my teachers knew that not everyone is as happy as they seem. Growing up my mother always had high expectations for my siblings and I. Going to school, then, coming home to cook and clean was never easy. My mother would always tell me, "Npaj Koj lub neej kom zoo, es lawm hnub koj thiaj mus ua ib tug nyab zoo." In English, she said, "prepare for your life now, so that one day you'll be a good wife." Now that I'm older, I cherish those golden words.

My mother was a single parent of nine kids. She was *ib sab niam ib sab txiv*, half mom and half dad, filling both shoes. She would work 60+ hours a week at a minimum wage of $13.50 and still managed to put food on the table and a roof over our heads. With the little we had, my mother saved so on our birthdays, we would get a small cake and a bag of chips, and if we're lucky enough, we would get two bags of chips. Even when we received the littlest gifts of love, she still managed to put a smile on our face, just knowing how hard she worked just to celebrate our birthdays every year. Growing up my mother was the most important person in my life. As I grew older I started to realize how much my mother is willing to sacrifice just for my health and education. And for that I owe my mother my life.

I was never the perfect student that received a 4.0 GPA on every report card. I was never the student who talked a lot in my class and when I knew the answer to the question on the board, I was the girl who never had enough courage to raise my hand to answer the question. I was mostly quiet due to having a lot of things on my plate or too many things going through my mind at once.

Sixth grade was the lowest point of my life. It was when I started to hate myself and I started to doubt myself. I thought I wasn't being my best, I thought that one day I would let my mother down painfully and that was my worst nightmare. I was those types of people who would keep everything to themselves and just let all the negativity sink in. And it got to the point where it started to devour me, not physically, but mentally. It wasn't hard to tell someone how I felt, but no one asked if I was okay. Family, teachers, counselors, and friends, no one notice how much I was suffering. I find it astonishing that some people, including me, would be hurting painfully inside, but still managing to cover everything up with just a single smile.

At that time, I felt so alone. I felt like it was just me against the world. It felt like I was drowning, drowning in my own thoughts, and no matter how hard I tired to fight this, I couldn't. All I needed was a just a single hand. I went through a lot growing up, mentally and physically.

Now that I have grown up and am in high school, my biggest goal is to graduate high school and go to a 4-year college for psychology. I want to study psychology personally because of what I went through and I feel like no one should ever feel that way. This is my story.

Sincerely,
Future Psychologist

CRIED MY HEART OUT

Dear Teacher,

I wish you knew that I'm not always that happy and cute Asian student with straight A's, but I'm still that bright and kind student you have known throughout the years. So here I am today, to share with you my struggles and my journey through my 17 years of life.

First, I'm the the oldest daughter and being the oldest daughter in a Hmong family carries many responsibilities. In the Hmong culture, the females are to succeed the parents' expectations. As the oldest daughter, I'm always expected to keep my grades as A's to be seen as a smart and perfect daughter, and I'm also expected to be perfect in cleaning and cooking no matter what. I find it hard to achieve these goals of theirs because not every human is perfect. At the end of the day, you will let them down somehow because humans are not perfect. In the Hmong community, status and first impression are a very big deal. In my family I was never allowed to speak or express myself from six-years-old until now because I was only seen as a child and that is why I grew up having trouble expressing myself. I was never given the permission to express myself, and I would always argue with my parents for not letting me express myself. Growing up, I got tired of being treated like I was just another person who gets used to accomplish someone else's needs and goals, which wasn't something I wanted to do because I know at the end of the day, the one who is going to be happy is them and not me. I became more frustrated with things like this, that I started to become more rebellious. I talked back with my parents trying only to express myself, and I ran away from home a couple of times and got into trouble.

Secondly, during middle school was when everything changed. I was going through a lot of mental health. I didn't know what to do with these thoughts and feelings of mine. I thought that if I showed up to school with a smile on my face, maybe I can forget things? But it was harder to forget, and people would misunderstand me even more because they thought I was this little girl who lived happily everyday.

Lastly, entering into high school my thoughts and feelings were rarely settled down during my freshman and sophomore year. In my freshman year, my family problems were only growing bigger, but I bottled them up because I thought it was one way for me to grow stronger. One day at the tennis courts after school, I just couldn't stay strong no more; it was just so tiring and stressful that for the first the time in awhile I cried so hard, I cried all my heart out pushing all those pain that I had bottled up over the years. After crying, it was refreshing, and I felt like I can do better that I can become a stronger person than I used to. Of course, my family problems continued, but I try to stay away from situations that don't involve me.

Sophomore year was the hardest thing for me because I had lost my best friend; she was more than just a friend, she was like a sister to me. You may think that she is just a best friend but watching each other learn and grow up together has so much meaning to me. What made her so important and valuable was because I put my happiness on her. That day when she left, I fell apart, but as time goes by I have learned to live happily. Now I have continuously met people that are even more amazing then the people that I have met in my past. Now, I'm a very happy girl. I'm 17-years-old and still have a lot to learn and have come so far.

Over all, I hope this will give you an idea of what kind of student

I used to be and a kind of student I'm now. I also hope that my story can help you connect with other students too.

Sincerely,
Cried My Heart Out

HEAVY SHOULDERS

Dear Teacher,

There are many times in my life where I wished a teacher would understand me as an individual, where my life at school to home can and may differ. The stress from late night studies. The negative thoughts that run across my mind multiple times, this is where it all started: high school.

As the baby in the house full of older siblings, I was looked up to for being the hopeful and only one that can and will finish high school. Our family was the center of attention for having a sibling who had a child at a young age, and some siblings who used to be in gangs. My parents compared me, every bit of me to my bones, to all my cousins, saying that I would be able to do it because my siblings couldn't. I wished my teacher understood that they, too, looked down on me because I don't seem to show effort in school due to what that I lacked in a certain subject. They even had me redo a required class to make myself look good. Hearing the same words from both school and home, I struggled to focus on studying. If only they knew I studied so hard to just understand a packet of homework teachers handed me.

Throughout my high school years, I would say that I have spent more the 5 hours at night studying. After a 4-5-hour shift at work, I would come home to study for another 4-5. Not only do I stress from studying, I would have to stress about when I will get my next meal to eat the following day. Not living with my parents gives me doubts in everything. I would come home to nothing but an empty place, a place I have to call a "home." I wake up for school the next day, knowing it's other day. My teachers don't even bother to see the signs of a student in need, thinking that I'm okay with everything in my life. Really, all I want is a day to relax and have someone ask me if I was "okay." Especially when, all I think about is that my life wouldn't have to be like this, if I wasn't alive.

Eventually, I started my sophomore year with scars up under my long sleeves. School and home took the best of me. I started to cut my friends out of my life and became alone. Once, a teacher saw my arms with my scars. They told me, "self-harm is not the way to go", never knowing the reason why I did that. Some simply say, "depression is all in your head." Those words run through my brain every time when someone tells me, "you'll be okay." Those words coming from teachers that simply didn't know me or even bother to listen to me. If only they knew that my family brings me down, my school thinks I'm useless, and that I have lost all the joy in my life to make others happy, then I wouldn't have the thoughts I have. I would be able to stop them from happening, if I was good enough, smart enough, and more selfish to think of myself.

Overall, I wished you understand me because I didn't mean to fail my tests. I didn't mean to let my family's thoughts overthrow me at 14. I studied hard, but what you are teaching, it doesn't make any sense to me. I lose my sleep to understand your lessons. I don't need you to tell me, "it's all in my head," when really you should be asking if I'm okay.

Sincerely,
Heavy Shoulders

STRONG FEMINIST

Dear Teacher,

It has been 1 year since I have last written a letter to you. I'm still really tired, but I'm working on getting a better night's rest. A lot has happened within a year. Surprisingly? My concern on marrying a Yang is no longer a problem because I don't think I will marry a Hmong man. Unless it starts raining pigs. I know my dad wouldn't agree with me on this, but I just feel Hmong men are just full of baloney. My life as a Hmong girl has always been a constant struggle because of Hmong men. This is my perspective on gender inequality in my community; you can take it with a grain of salt.

When there are parties, the women do all the cooking and cleaning. Hmong girls are forced to wake up at 5am in the morning to go cook, to prep food for a bunch of men that have their own legs and arms, who are able to cook for themself. No, they just sit at a big table while we serve them food and take their plates away. At the end of the the day, we get a simple, "Thank you." If you were really thankful, you would do more than say a simple, "thank you." You would make room at the table for us women you would let us in on the conversation. You think women wouldn't understand. I know some of these men are old and traditional, but half of the other men are in their late 30's and early 40's. Come on they are old enough to understand that this is not how women, or any human should be treated. The Hmong culture is honestly really messed-up because there is too much toxic masculinity.

This summer my cousin was in a tragic car accident and passed away. The weekend of her funeral, I almost couldn't go because of the clan picnic, which my dad was the host of and so it was a big deal to him. I told my mom that a dumb clan picnic comes around every year but seeing my cousin for one last time is final. My dad said that she was young, so we don't need to go to her funeral meaning she wasn't an important person. Just because she didn't seem like an important person to elders, doesn't mean she wasn't important to other people. Just because she was a child, doesn't mean she doesn't deserve respect.

When the funeral arrived, my father changed his mind to attend on Sunday morning because the clan picnic was on Saturday. I went earlier on Saturday morning till later at night, and I wanted to stay longer, but couldn't. I thought it was really dumb that my dad went. I was the one that cared to be there. He went so that his "image" would look good. He went to pay respect, but really it was just a fake cover, so he looks like a good son-in-law.

I love my dad, but at times I wish he would just stop and look at his family and see we need him. We have billions of cousins who he always spends time with, organizing events, attending meetings, and celebrations. His family is with his little girls, so they need their father figure too because I didn't have him and I always felt something's missing. When I was younger my mom got divorce, so from my early ages there was no one to call daddy in my life.

Throughout the Hmong men I have met, there are only a few good ones, but the rest are just a disappointment to the gender of men. I know that not all Hmong men are bad, but how do I know they are good? Young Hmong boys can change the future; they can change to become less like the traditional Hmong men. I hate it when some Hmong men think a woman are their slave. It's hard to believe people think this way still, but I think Hmong culture is worse than you think it already is.

P.S - I'm trying to find the beauty within the Hmong culture because I know Hmong people are better than this.

Sincerely,
Strong Feminist

HAD THE WORLD'S BEST UNCLE

Dear Teacher,

I'm new to Park Center. I'm from California and I have been moving my entire life. I have been to 8 schools in 16 years. I was born in Fresno, California and then moved to Merced, California when I was four or five. I spent my entire life in California up until I was thirteen, then my dad decided to move from Merced to Mankato, Minnesota. Just this summer I moved to Brooklyn Park, Minnesota. I have been living in Minnesota for 3 years now and here is what I wish you knew about me.

In first grade I went to school at North Green Elementary School. I loved it there. My uncle Kou lived with my family and I at the time. He was like any other uncle; he teased me all the time, but at the end of the day, he tried to give me all the love he could give. I never thought anything about it at the time since I was so innocent and naive, but my uncle always wore blue. He wore blue bandanas, blue hats, blue shirts, etc. One night my uncle went out and my little brother asked where he was going. "I'm going to my friend's house, I will be right back though okay? Bye Coco," and with a smile my uncle turned around and left.

That night I woke up to my mom waking me up abruptly. I don't remember how we got in the car, but somehow all of my family and I were in our red Ford SUV and driving to an unknown neighborhood. As we approached our destination, red and blue flashing lights became even brighter and brighter. I sat, frightened and silent in the car with my siblings as my mom and dad stepped out to talk to the police. I don't remember what happened after that, but the next morning my parents told me my uncle had been shot and killed.

My uncle got into the wrong crowd as he grew up. Being a Hmong refugee, he didn't have many options, so eventually he just fell into the wrong crowd. There was nothing that could be done to change his fate. So, we grieved and we let time heal us. That is all for now. Until next time.

Sincerely,
Had the World's Best Uncle

Final Words

Thank you for reading these letters. We hope that they have touched your hearts the same way they have touched ours. Our sincere wish is that our students feel valued for who they are and what they represent: their past, their present, and their future. We believe that this project has shown our students the significance of their voices and we hope that they feel empowered to continue in this journey of self-discovery each and every day.

This all began with one teacher sharing her story of who she was and how she felt as a Hmong American teenager. She wanted to show her students that they were not alone. It has grown into so much more. May you find authentic ways to connect with your students and learn from them just as they learn from us.

Here are some resources that might help in connecting with your Hmong students and their families:
- Hmong Health Care Professional Coalition - https://www.facebook.com/HHCPC/
- Wilder Foundation Hmong Mental Health Services: https://www.wilder.org/
- Hmong Cultural Center - https://www.hmongcc.org/

- Hmong Museum - http://hmongmuseummn.org
- Hmong Cultural Guide, Center for Advanced Studies in Child Welfare (CASCW), University of Minnesota - https://cascw.umn.edu/wp-content/uploads/2014/04/CulturalGuide-Hmong.pdf
- Hmong Archive - https://hmongarchives.org/
- Hmong American Partnership - http://www.hmong.org/
- Hmong Educational Resource Publisher - https://herpublisher.com
- Minnesota Public Radio (MPR) article, "10 things about Hmong culture, food and language you probably didn't know" https://www.mprnews.org/story/2015/03/01/10-things-hmong
- Mindset Works - https://www.mindsetworks.com/parents/school-home-connection

Strategies to get your students talking/sharing/writing/collaborating:
- Inside/Outside circle
- Clock partners
- Pen pals/journal partners
- Using technology - creating podcasts, blogs, hyperdocs
- Writing fiction and non-fiction books
- Individualized Learning/Student choice (path, place, and pace) for assignments
- Regular opportunities to practice
- Ungraded writing assignments
- Conversation circles